EBURY PRESS

HOW TO BE A LIKEABLE BIGOT

Naomi Datta is a creative director, presenter and writer with a number of leading channels. She is the author of the satirical *The 6 P.M. Slot* published by Penguin Random House India. Naomi is a frequent and widely followed commentator on mass culture through her Twitter handle nowme_datta and her columns in various publications.

HOW TO BE A LIKEABLE BIGOT

A HANDBOOK FOR THE SAVVY SURVIVOR

NAOMI DATTA

EBURY
PRESS

An imprint of Penguin Random House

EBURY PRESS

USA | Canada | UK | Ireland | Australia
New Zealand | India | South Africa | China | Singapore

Ebury Press is part of the Penguin Random House group of companies
whose addresses can be found at global.penguinrandomhouse.com

Published by Penguin Random House India Pvt. Ltd
4th Floor, Capital Tower 1, MG Road,
Gurugram 122 002, Haryana, India

First published in Ebury Press by Penguin Random House India 2019

Illustrations by Saurabh Deb

ISBN 9780143447146

Typeset in Berling LT Std Manipal Technologies Limited, Manipal

Printed at Repro India Limited

www.penguin.co.in

For my husband, Adrian, who would never otherwise read a book on being a proactive slacker

Contents

1. How to Contribute Nothing to Team Meetings
   and Not Let Anyone Catch On   1

2. How to Make Your Résumé Work Harder
   than You   17

3. How to Spend All Your Time on Social
   Media and Yet Give the Illusion of Productivity   31

4. How to Be a Gainfully Occupied Freeloader   43

5. How to Be Unfit and Be Morally Superior OR
   How to Be Fit and Not Invite Resentment   55

6. Mummy Politics for the Dummy   63

7. How to Be a Kangaroo Dad
   (How to Contribute Nothing to Parenting and
   Yet Be Dad of the Year)   79

8. How to Be a Likeable Bigot   93

9. How to Be a Sulking Liberal   111

10. How to Be a Chronic Feel-gooder   123

11. How to Be a Journalist and Never Report
    on Anything   137

12. How to Crack Woke Jokes   149

13. How to Be Casually Sexist   159

14. How to Be a Sports Legend without
    Ever Getting Injured   167

15. How to Escape Reality and Live in
    a Parallel Timeline of Your Own   181

Select Bibliography   189
Acknowledgements   191

How to Contribute Nothing to Team Meetings and Not Let Anyone Catch On

There is nothing more depressing than an office—for a shallow, insular person, that is. Because if you are not that, you would know that there are far more acute crises of humanity than a listless workplace. But if you are not the self-contained wallflower sitting on the fence that this book is primarily for, then you must exit immediately. You have stumbled upon the wrong book. Stop right here and burn your copy—but make sure to document it on Instagram with a suitably woke hashtag. You could have a conscience and still be an exhibitionist; the two would be a perfect Tinder match.

Workplaces, even those where they put in beanbags and have beer Fridays for their employees, are designed to trigger gloom. There is a certain type of employee who likes going into work; there is even a personality type for it. It is called the Type A personality: a combative, ambitious and incredibly annoying office worker. In some cause for comfort, the Type A is apparently more at risk of heart disease than most. Type As don't intend to be employees for long; they are the ones you can count on to set up loss-making start-ups with high valuations.

Then there is the Type B: the relaxed, affable chap who sooner or later will take off to become a yoga teacher and write long-form blogs on connecting his chakras. You don't want to be this guy either. You actually don't want a personality type because the aim is to not have a personality. You need to be a blur of vague congeniality: when people try to draw a mental image of you, it should be a pleasant haze. This will ensure that you always stay under the radar. This also means that glory will elude you, but you won't get taken down either. The aim is to proactively sideline yourself. In your obscurity, you are self-made.

Now, of course, all this sounds great on paper. But it needs work and a plan. I present a multipronged approach to guide your ascent into corporate oblivion. This approach will cover two broad work hubs: offline and online. Offline largely comprises meetings with human beings in the flesh and conference calls with disembodied human beings. Online encompasses emails and WhatsApp work groups. Both these spaces are equally important, so make sure to exercise due vigilance.

First, the offline aspect.

In team meetings, place yourself next to the person who you know will take the lead in the meeting. This will always be the Type A with the wilting heart that he or she is not yet aware of. Be old-school—carry a notepad and pen and take copious notes. Always offer to send the minutes of the meeting. When you seat yourself in such close proximity to the leader, the chances of getting stared down are minimized. Type A will stare down the table or across the table. Craning his or her neck sideways to stare down genial note-taker has no swag. When Type A is preoccupied with staring down assorted colleagues, make sure to smile sympathetically and subtly at them. Just a tiny, almost indiscernible twitch of the lips and narrowing of the eyes; don't overdo it. You have empathy, but you have cast your lot with management. The few times Type A deigns to look your way, don't be too enthusiastic. Cultivate an expression of contemplative appreciation as opposed to fawning adulation. This expression entails the tiniest of frowns and slightly parted lips, accompanied by imperceptible nods. Now, a note of caution: you are not a sycophant. A sycophant has defined character traits; you must have none. A brown-noser is generally despised. Your aim is to not evoke any excess emotion. Showing neither adulation nor contempt, you must entrench yourself in the realm of indifference. Once the meeting is over, send out detailed minutes. This brings us to the next crucial weapon in our arsenal: emails.

They are just four words, four words so simple that they exist even in the vocabulary of a preschooler. These four glorious words are: PUT IT ON EMAIL. If words could kill time, this phrase would be a serial killer. It has single-handedly destroyed hours, weeks, even months of human activity and has brought down civilizations. You will action this descent into the black hole of email communication. Please note that this is the only time you will show initiative, but it is for a larger cause: initiative to bring about inertia. It isn't rocket science, but it could be physics. Every action has an equal and opposite reaction. By proactively setting off an email chain, you are bringing about extended inactivity. It looks like a lot of activity, but its marginal productivity is zero. They have a term for this in high-school economics: disguised unemployment. PFB (please find below; always use official-sounding acronyms) a sample email. Pointers are provided in *italics*.

To: The Whole World
CC: Boss
Subject: Minutes of the Meeting
Date: 15 August 2018

Dear all,

As discussed, here are the main points covered today. We have chalked out a roadmap and I am quickly putting down the milestones with actionable points. Please do let me know if I have missed anything.

Blah blah blah expedite. Growth trajectory blah blah blah. Blah blah leverage blah blah.

(Use 'leverage' in EVERY email. You could be asking for a day's leave, but you should say you would like to take a day off to leverage opportunities for personal work.

Put down about ten bullet points. They should say the same thing in different ways. Try and use words such as 'ameliorate' and 'amalgam'. And now for the masterstroke. Towards the end of the email, drop in the line below.)

Do revert with your thoughts by EOD.

(EOD is a bit like GOD. It is omniscient, much revered, but no one has really seen it. EOD is also a paradox of time. It signifies a finite period of time that can actually stretch to infinity.)

Best,
Obscure Genial Person

Now sit back and watch the fun. Type A will find it tough to resist the power of his or her own thoughts now chronicled so astutely in long-winded pointlessness. Type A will respond first to each of your points with the legend 'my thoughts in red'. This will set off a mad scramble for colours. Wait for Type B to send in thoughts in a feeble pink. At this point, you will helpfully suggest that colleagues should stick to VIBGYOR—primary colours that underline the boldness of our thoughts. You, however, will stick to a value-neutral black. A riot of colours will ensue. As colour schemes are exhausted, people will forget why they were emailing each other in the first place. With some luck, a year will pass at the very least.

If at any time you discover that your scheme is floundering and some actual work is dangerously close to being done, you need to step in fast. Introduce the loop principle of managerial delegation. This entails introducing new characters in the cast to delay proceedings.

Here is what you need to do: 'Reply all' to the email and add a new recipient to the mix. Do this several times. As they say, you are getting so-and-so in the loop. So-and-so has no direct bearing or consequence on the matter being discussed, but these tactical additions are crucial. Here is a list of key people you can add at intervals whenever the discussion looks perilously close to a culmination:

+ Head of administration. This person is added when the discussion has moved on to the need for a meeting with key stakeholders. You loop this person in to raise a point regarding the copious amounts of coffee being consumed in times of cost-cutting.

+ Head of HR. The discussion has reached a stalemate. You question whether the already overworked team has the bandwidth for the matter at hand. You loop in the HR head to get in more resources.
+ Head of IT. You suggest a video conference amongst all branch offices. IT will now need to be looped in and a tangential subplot on connectivity can be successfully built upon.
+ New intern. To get a fresh Gen Z perspective. Say 'Gen Z', not 'young'. Only greenhorns call the young young.
+ Reception. 'Sometimes the best point of view can come from unexpected quarters' is how you sell this.
+ Pantry boy. This is critical; this is when you say the consensus approach has to be broad-based. Go down to the lowest common denominator.

The last email in this exchange can read thus if things go to plan:

To: The Whole World
CC: Boss
Subject: Re Minutes of the Meeting
Date: 25 August 2020

Dear all,

Just to get you up to speed on what the previous management team was contemplating, I have found the original minutes of the meeting and the 5000 emails that followed. Please do read the thread.

Let's discuss this COB or do send me your thoughts. Please pick VIBGYOR colours. We can collate and huddle soon.

Best,
Obscure Genial Person (*who survived the management overhaul from last week*)

(*NOTE: COB stands for close of business. You substitute EOD with COB lest anyone be daft enough to point out that you haven't had much personal growth in the years since that first email. That ought to teach them.*)

This now brings us to a crucial aspect of official communication: WhatsApp work groups and the interpersonal dynamics that you have to manage there. I haven't a clue how any work ever got done in a pre-WhatsApp era; I am convinced that nothing of note happened. Now, however, seriousness of intent is gauged by how quickly you set up a WhatsApp group for a project. Below are pointers on how to be proactive yet passive here.

1. Always be the Administrator. This is the first-mover advantage that will prove you are a person of intent

and initiative. Always offer to set up the group. The first thing you can do to slow down work is ask for a consensus on what the group should be called. Make it a bit of a cockfight (remember, Type A is part of this group and will want to slap his or her authority on it). Do also remember that a fair amount of brown-nosing is bound to happen; you need to avoid that temptation. You are not a sycophant. You are a survivor.

Example
You (Administrator): So, welcome to the new work group. Please let me know if I have missed anyone and send their numbers to me.

(Do not offer to share Administrator responsibilities with anyone else. That is a tactical advantage that we will cling to for the time being.

There will be a flurry of discussions on who has been missed out and whom to include. Let everyone get into a bit of an ego tussle over which of their subordinates they can include.)

You: Now that all key stakeholders are on the group, are we good with the name [Top Priority 101]? This will be our hundred-and-first top priority group in the space of two months. Good going, team.

Type B: It's nice, but it's kind of done. We should do something creative and lateral with the name.

Type A: (*a bit peeved that he or she didn't think of that but quickly takes charge*) Yes. Let's make it TP 101.

Sycophant: I love that. It retains the essence but gives it a no-nonsense air of business. We should totally go with TP 101. I feel the urgency. Go Team TP 101.

Person who never likes anything but never has an alternative: I just feel it doesn't sound right. I can't put my finger on it though. I am thinking, guys. I think we are almost there.

You: (typing, 'AE#21&>') (*You are just typing; you have no intention of sending the text.*)

Type B: Let it be something with soul. Work finally connects to our inner being. Let's call it Passion Project 101.

(*A flurry of clap emoticons floods the chat.*)

You: (Still typing, '@!13??/$%*#E')

Type A: Passion Project sounds like we are making porn, bro. Don't get me wrong. I love it. But in our business, messaging is everything. Happy to take this offline.

(*Now, as you know, Type B is benign and non-combative and will therefore give up the chase at the first sign of aggression. 'Happy to take it offline' is just the right veiled threat of potential physical aggression or worse, a sinister plan to spit in your coffee.*)

Type B: Now that you put it that way, TP 101 it is. No sweat.

You: I wrote this long message but just deleted it by mistake. What an idiot! (*The group has seen you 'typing' so they will believe you.*) But never mind. My thoughts were pretty much in the same vein. Let's do this!

(*You change the group name to TP 101. But you aren't quite done. Not enough time has been wasted, in your humble estimation.*)

You: You know what, I am including Young Person in this group so that we have an ear to the ground.

(Young Person is Cocky Intern Waiting to Leave for Yale Aka Progeny of Friend of Senior Management. You add Young Person. The group, which was a combination of swagger, sycophancy, stonewalling and subterfuge, now gets a heady touch of second-generation privilege and entitlement.)

You: Welcome, Young Person, to TP 101. Do let us know your perspective on the name of the group. Let's crack this first, guys. This is like the soul of the project. We get this right, the rest will follow. YP, your thoughts?

(YP takes two hours to check the notification.)

YP: Whoops. Just saw this. It's chill. What will Time Pass 101 do? Is it like a hobbies group? TP is so cute. My mum uses that a lot.

(Silence. You are typing.)

Type A: Let's just call it Top Priority 101. I was never convinced about TP 101.

Sycophant: Yes. It does reduce the no-nonsense air around it. Has no urgency.

Type B: *(Sends a folded-hands emoticon.)*

Thinker not doer: I am still not sure, but let's go with what we have. Could we maybe just like italicize Top? Gives it a bit of a slant.

(*Flurry of thumbs-up emoticons*)

Type A: It's a bit puff. The italics.

Sycophant: I agree. Looks non-serious.

Type B: It's not too bad. I kind of like it.

You: Sure. I think we should get in a few more voices. But for the time being we should call it Top Priority 101 WIP. Works?

I will not elaborate further but you see the pattern now. Don't stop till the group effectively becomes Top Priority 101 RIP.

2. Divide and rule. It isn't quite enough to form a solitary WhatsApp group. Now is your chance to create a complex web of frenetic activity, which is finally an elaborate labyrinth of nothingness. Within Top Priority 101, create subgroups. Top Priority 101 Core Team, Top Priority 101 Think Tank, Top Priority 101 Execution Team, Top Priority 101 R&D, Top Priority 101 Meeting Room Booking Team, Top

Priority 101 F&B. You will be the Administrator on all these groups and as a result, most of your workday will be spent in you looking hassled and busy. You don't have to contribute a single idea to any of these groups, but you will look like the most involved and conscientious team member. You will also set off intrigue and politicking as people vie to be part of the group that matters or be part of the maximum number of groups. You will remain a neutral Administrator, rising above petty plots for workplace domination.

3. Hyperventilate. WRITE IN CAPS. ALWAYS SOUND STRESSED. KEEP IT SIMPLE. SPELL IT OUT. I AM SO STRESSED. I REALLY NEED TO STOP OVER-INVESTING. I WAS DREAMING OF TOP PRIORITY 101 LAST NIGHT. WE ARE IN IT TOGETHER. GO TEAM TOP PRIORITY. Always sound like you are at the breaking point as you push yourself past every imaginable limit set by humanity on WhatsApp group Administrators.

4. Send messages at unearthly hours. Make sure to send messages to the group at odd hours to appear ever alert and wakeful. The messages don't have to be of any import, but will shame the rest of the group as they try to sleep, eat or do anything apart from Top Priority 101.

These are some simple rules in the art of managing WhatsApp groups at work. These principles will differ for different units—parents, families, housing societies, school friends. We will delve into that as well. But for now, just remember one key rule: never share your Administrator responsibilities with anyone. Never ever. Ever.

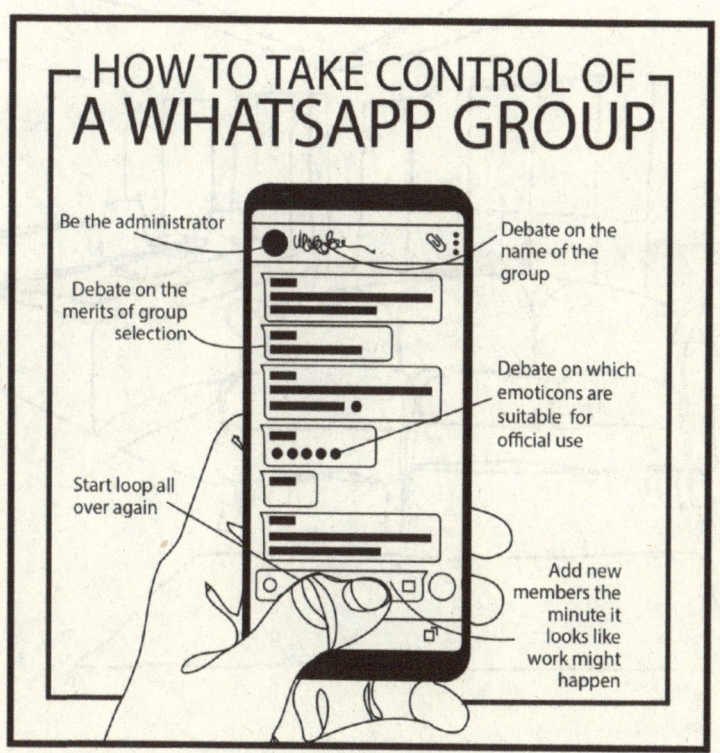

HOW TO TAKE CONTROL OF
A WHATSAPP GROUP

Be the administrator

Debate on the name of the group

Debate on the merits of group selection

Debate on which emoticons are suitable for official use

Start loop all over again

Add new members the minute it looks like work might happen

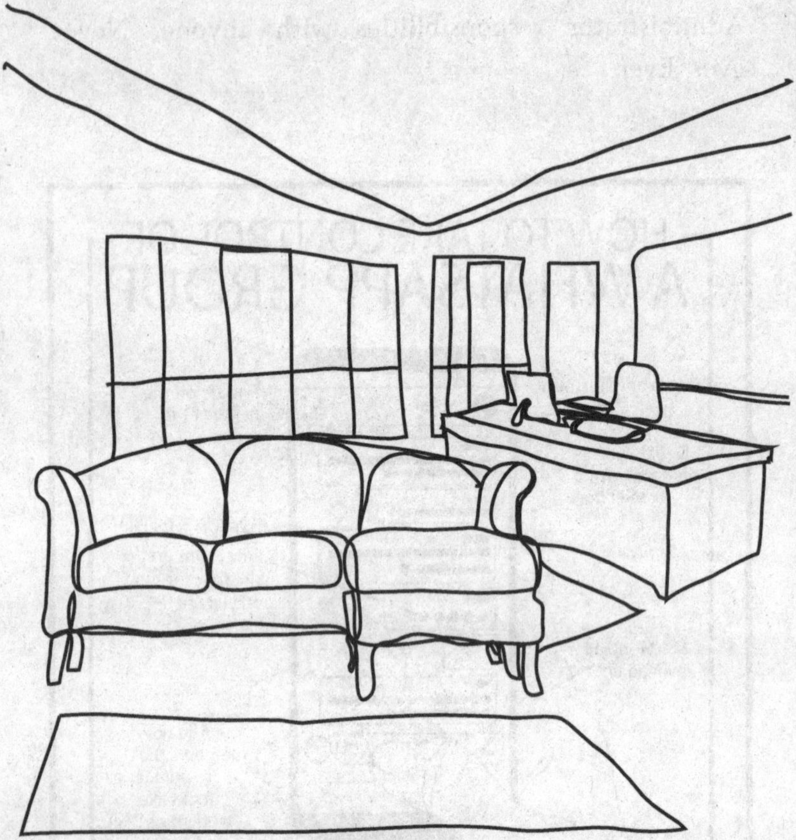

2

How to Make Your Résumé Work Harder than You

The aim of this book is to set you up as a non-achieving, complacent fence-sitter at the very least and a stonewaller at the very best. But I don't want you to be poor or a failure. I would have written a book on optimizing spiritual health then. You are a mass of inertia, but your career will always be on a steady ascendant. Not a meteoric rise, because as we will say ad nauseam throughout this book, you don't want to be noticed too much. Your career goal is to be furniture in your workplace. However, you can choose to be the plush couch in the lobby rather than the plastic chair left out in the rain.

Our key objective is to stay in one organization for as long as possible—stay the course, survive management changes, blend in, be seen as a company loyalist and inveigle yourself into some kind of mid-senior managerial post. That is ideal. You are the person who throws the rule book at new employees and resists all change by saying that it is against the brand values of the company. 'This is not who we are,' you repeat in tones of deep anguish each time something pops up that could topple the apple cart, your apple cart. Apples are odious fruits just by the way they fall unsolicited on people and make them come up with laws of gravity. The interfering busybodies encourage thought and change. You are a fruit for god's sake. Behave like one. Give me a complacent plum any day.

But we digress. While the above state of ennui will work for as long as we can make it work, we have to have a backup plan. There might come a time when you will need to relocate the couch to different premises. You don't need to change what the couch is fundamentally, but you will have to tinker with the upholstery. You will have to refurbish it and make it look and sound more productive than it is or ever was.

What is the job definition of a couch? A couch is 'a long upholstered piece of furniture for several people to sit on'. This is at the core of what a couch stands for. This is what a truthful, honest couch would say if it applied to move to another organization.

How would I rate the chances of the aforesaid truthful couch getting alternative, higher-paying employment? Fat. Sorry, not fat. Body positive but non-existent. At most, they will enlist the couch and put it in the recycling department at a lower pay scale. In other words, scrap it.

But what if the couch defined its role like this instead:

Executive summary: Was in a leadership role in the lobby of my previous organization. The other pieces of furniture were aligned and designed around the philosophy I set in place. I was a custodian of brand values: I set the mood and feel of the organization as I was the first thing people noticed when they walked in. I would describe myself as ergonomic. I encouraged both diversity and inclusiveness as different people sought comfort while sitting on me. I also set the note for aspiration: if visitors were guided to me, it meant they had *arrived*.

You see what happened here? The couch goes from being a generic piece of furniture to a custodian of brand tonality and a people aggregator. The couch gets hired and will now occupy a prime place in the CEO's office. If you haven't got it yet, the couch is you. It is a metaphor for you. This chapter is not about finding an alternative employment for couches. It is about employment options for you. Though, some would say that a couch and you are pretty much the same thing. A mildly disrespectful view, which happens to be true.

So this is what we need to do now. We need to spin a web of subterfuge, mild deceit, white lies, intrigue and posturing. In other words, we have to get your CV or résumé in place—and additionally a LinkedIn profile. A piece of advice: I would save the money on a premium membership for LinkedIn. That way you can imagine that people of great clout and consequence are stalking your profile. Reality could prove to be cruel.

Coming back to your documented work profile, the full form of CV is curriculum vitae, which is Latin for 'the course of your life'. 'Résumé' and 'CV' are often used interchangeably, but that is not entirely correct. A CV is a more elaborate, comprehensive description of your professional life and academic experience. A résumé, on the other hand, is a concise summary of your work experience and should ideally not go beyond one page. For the purposes of our chapter, we will focus on the résumé because no employer actually reads beyond a page in any case, if at all.

There are some ground rules for résumés, which are pretty standard and non-negotiable.

1. Be concise. Be crisp and use short sentences. Keep puns and verse for your blog.
2. Choose a readable font and clean template. Don't use fancy designs and colours. Your résumé is not an adult colouring book.
3. Be a grammar vigilante. Please don't say you are a grammar Nazi, ever. Don't say you are any kind of Nazi, ever. This is a book about likeable, ineffectual and mildly awful people.
4. Spellcheck like your life depends on it.

That then is the skeleton of your résumé. Now for the part where we get creative. We don't lie; we employ creative techniques of storytelling. Think of your career as a Bollywood biopic and your résumé as the trailer. We can't let reality interfere too much. We have to loosely base the résumé on your actual life and then creatively alter the details. We will try not to change your gender, but apart from that, everything is par for the course. There will be no outright lies, just little embellishments to spruce up your professional achievements. Like an item song in a film without a plot. Do note that while we are being creative in structuring your résumé, we are not using 'creative' to describe you. Apparently, internal studies done by LinkedIn show that it is the third-most overused word across profiles.

Here are some words that should definitely find their way into your résumé. We will figure context later and retrofit the narrative. But these words/terms are mandatory. Memorize them.

1. Maven. A maven is a person with good knowledge or understanding of a subject. It somehow (and this is not in the dictionary) also gives the implicit impression of being a maverick. Don't use maverick to describe yourself, though. It is much too presumptuous. Instead, arm-twist someone else to write you a recommendation using that word. Like a junior whose promotion depends on your good office.

2. Ideas curator/aggregator. You have never actually had an original idea in your life but are really good at filching ideas. Which means that you have the elusive ability to detect a good idea and then pass it off as

your own. You were made for senior management. Go ahead and describe yourself as an ideas curator.

3. Thought leader. You have never held a position of leadership in your workplace, but you do have the ability to guide thoughts and lead them in the right direction—your own thoughts, nobody else's as no one else cares two hoots about you. But you don't need to mention that. For the purposes of your résumé, you are a thought leader.

4. Digital evangelist. You can use 'evangelist' on its own as well, but attaching digital to anything automatically makes it sound modern and cutting-edge. An evangelist is a passionate advocate for something, so if you are the most passionate setter-up of work WhatsApp groups, you are a digital evangelist.

5. Verticals. Don't use 'departments' to describe your area of work unless you actually work in a department store. Always say you drove growth across xyz verticals. It doesn't matter if you don't head the vertical. Being a growth-driver across verticals makes you sound like a multitasker and versatile person. Sanjay Manjrekar could have called Ravindra Jadeja a growth-driver across verticals instead of a 'bits-and-pieces player' and saved himself a lot of trouble.

6. Employer aggrandizer. This is just a lot of babble, but it sounds incredibly important. It implies that you empower your employer by enhancing his or her reputation. It basically means that you are a

consummate yes-man. Potential employers love hiring yes-men who manage to give the impression of being independent thinkers.

7. Process disrupter. It's a new world out there—one that believes it is constantly reinventing the wheel. It isn't actually, but you don't need to tell anyone that. However, potential employers must feel that you are the disruptive force that will bring about this change. You are the kind of subversive subordinate that every company that actually doesn't want freethinkers wants. You are a person who shakes up processes by adding more processes. You don't need to define which process you disrupted; it could be that you decided PowerPoints should not end on a vanilla slide that says 'Thank You', but should reflect the brand philosophy and motto of the company and should rather end with a slide that says, 'Be the Change You Want to Be'. This is a huge systemic and attitudinal change in the organization and you should take full credit for it.

8. Initiative incubator. Start-up incubators are a bit passé and involve actual work. An initiative incubator, on the other hand, is just someone who gets others to initiate things, which could be anything. Keep the initiative open-ended and ambiguous. Like initiating a stamp collection club or a B-movie screening club. The initiative needn't have anything to do with work. In fact, it is recommended that it have nothing to do with work, ever.

9. Activity hacker. You are being truthful here. You are the person who ensures that no actual activity ever happens. But the term suggests quite the opposite. You are the person who accelerates growth and activity. You are an engine for growth.

10. Happiness hero. This term is used when you are in HR and are trying to find meaning in your overly administrative job. You actually have no say in the policies of the company and are just a pen-pusher. Your most vital decision-making in the year was to give female employees paraben-free make-up on Women's Day—which backfired as a sexist and divisive move. You now send birthday emails every day to employees and have redesignated yourself as a happiness hero. The only person you are giving happiness to is yourself.

The above, then, is a glossary of power words that can make your résumé stand out from the glut of résumés with hackneyed clichés such as team player, people skills, passionate, motivated, self-driven, lateral thinker, off-centrist problem-solving. These are much too mundane and banal. Avoid all these unimaginative terms.

Our work is not done yet. I will now demonstrate how you can use the words we have discussed to construct a potent résumé. Not the entire résumé, but at least the executive summary. I forgot to mention: write your résumé in the third person. It sounds like you had a management team write it for you. You are that much of a cool customer.

Example A

Suresh has never lasted beyond a year and a half in any job. He moves from start-up to start-up, is smart enough to realize when the funds are drying up and exits the sinking ship. He is a slacker and is probably the guy who capsized the ship to begin with. He is adept at handling bosses—he remembers the birthdays of their distant cousins and sends flowers.

Executive Summary: Suresh has always demonstrated the ability to be ahead of the curve in the exciting world of technology start-ups. An activity hacker, he is a risk-taker with a nose for sniffing out entrepreneurial gumption. In a diverse career, Suresh has always believed in aggrandizing his employers and senior management. As a technology maven, his is a truly empowered vision.

Example B

Paromita has been in the same organization for ten years. She is comfortable, complacent and completely closed to new ideas. A dreadful gossip, she spends most of her time politicking. Her big power move was when she got the office to also stock sugar-free equivalents. This was the one time she decided to go on a diet. The diet was abandoned—the sugar-free stays. Nobody, including Paromita, has figured out what she is good at and she is constantly moved across departments.

Executive Summary: Paromita is a believer in company values and is a brand custodian. An ideas aggregator, she is a process disruptor. Her contribution to work processes and flows that optimize resources extends even to the lowest link, the pantry. Paromita is a growth-driver across many verticals and each has benefited from her domain expertise.

· You get the gist? This is how you get your résumé to work harder for you. Do note that a résumé is now no longer just a piece of paper: if it isn't digital, it isn't working. Therefore, presence on social networking websites is mandatory. However, try not to use LinkedIn as an extension of your Instagram feed and keep your vacation photographs to Facebook. Your personality on LinkedIn is corporate, congenial and always about a learning that you can use in your job or to better yourself professionally.

Let me illustrate how the same event can be portrayed differently on different social media forums and how you can juggle your multiple personality disorder on social media.

Case: Kane Williamson's New Zealand team loses in a dramatic World Cup cricket final to England. The two teams were tied, but New Zealand finally lost thanks to a bizarre technicality.

You (on Twitter): Damn it! This is bizarre. Trust England to win on a technicality. Typical. #DownWithTheICC

(This is your evil, toxic twin.)

You (on Instagram with a photo of Kane): #Noble #NiceGuysFinishFirst #HeartBreak #EpicFinal #NeverForget #Emotional #YouWonOurHearts #ServesYouRightForBeatingIndia.

Okay. Maybe not the last one.

(This is the schmaltzy Hallmark version to impress potential dates.)

You (on Facebook): This was an epic final—was watching it with a roomful of people and was hoarse cheering the men in black. Gutted. New Zealand wins our hearts.

(This is your regulation, everyday Everyman persona.)

You (on LinkedIn): In record time, you turn around a post/blog on *The Rule Book: why playing by the rules is the disruption your business needs. Ten insights from the World Cup final.*

(This is you bright-eyed and bushy-tailed, prowling the corporate world, ready for the kill.)

The insights can be banal and pedestrian, but your ability to turn a topical event into a life lesson that will benefit your peer group and yourself will be appreciated. Remember, LinkedIn is nothing but a lot of earnest bunkum and humble bragging. You are constantly weighed down by the sheer volume of your achievement. Your overarching humility can barely keep up with your accomplishments. It is a good place to be. It is infinitely humbling. Almost every day, something in your professional life triggers a wave of humility and you make a note of it on your work profile.

1. Humbled that the building watchman noticed I am always so late coming back from work. Humbled by his generosity of spirit. He is awake a lot more than me.
2. Humbled that my school WhatsApp group found a clipping of my new job announcement and posted it on the group. The love of old friends who think of your accomplishments as their own is humbling.
3. Humbled to have met the Chairman and have him give us a thumbs-up on targets achieved. Blessed to be working with a team that supports me in everything I do. I know I am a bit impossible, but with you guys, everything seems possible. Humbled that you repose so much faith in me.

On that note, I must humbly submit that you are now all set for a productive career in slacking off. Simply follow the infinite wisdom set out in this chapter and gently glide along unbothered by exigencies of any kind.

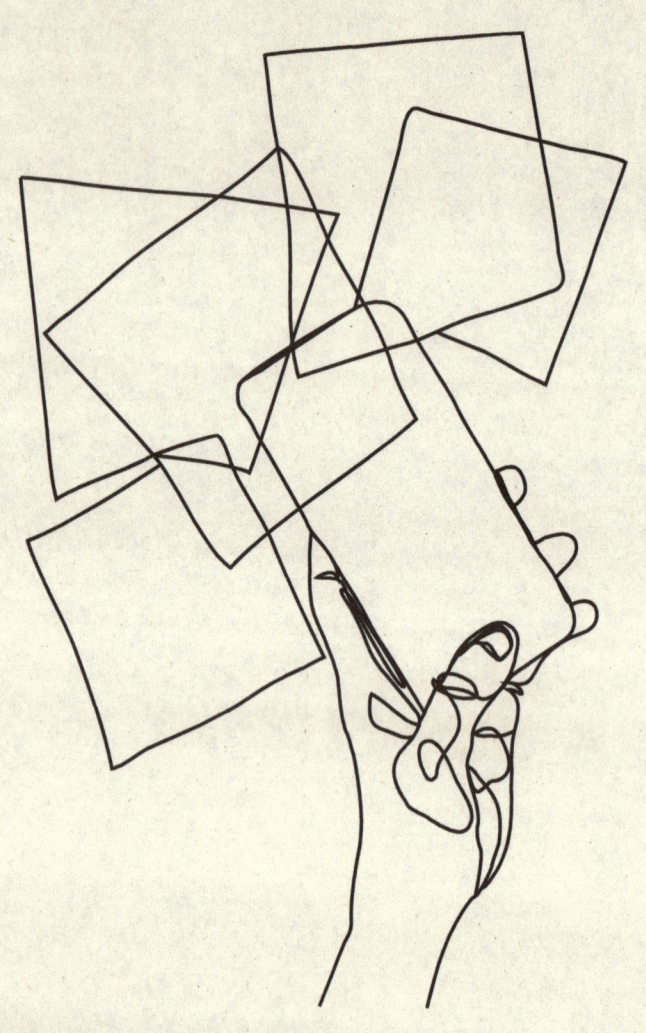

3

How to Spend All Your Time on Social Media and Yet Give the Illusion of Productivity

If you are on social media a lot, you are unemployed. Or you are a journalist who is tracking what Twitter says on a wide range of subjects. Which is as good as being unemployed because that really *isn't* a job or even journalism. Or you are an influencer making money off of your sponsored posts; then again, you are not much of an influencer if you are doing it on your own. Really important influencers have agencies and agents—and if you are reading this, there is no way you have an agent, or are likely to.

Now that we have established that you are the proactively unambitious person that this book caters to, let's work on your image. You must wonder: Why does a person who has pretty much abdicated ambition need an image? Please note the usage of 'proactively' in a previous line. It was deliberate. It won't do for the outside world to know the depths of complacency to which you have sunk. We still need to pay bills and nobody hires complacent, closed individuals. Actually, they do all the time, but complacent, closed individuals make sure that no one catches on to their true nature. So, we proactively remain inactive. We create illusions, and that, friends, is the hardest work we will ever do.

Enter the forces of social media. Since we have established that you are a person whose default setting is stonewalling, we are now going to extrapolate wildly. You are also a person who spends a lot of time on social media given that you have a lot of time to spare. And the reason you have a lot of time to spare is that you spend a large part of your existence making sure you have a lot of time to spare. But even a stonewaller needs something to occupy them, and that could well be your Facebook wall.

Your FB wall is not a wall; it is a well of nothingness. A deep, dark bottomless well that can subsume you, consume you. Take up every waking moment you have—and it is perfect to constantly lower the bar on achievement. But herein lies the challenge: how can you spend all your time on social media and yet ensure that you come across as a self-motivated individual? Here is a step-by-step guide on how not to look idle on social media—an oxymoron if ever there was one.

Be Well-Referenced

You don't need to be well-read. The key is to be well-referenced. Post links to articles on a wide variety of topics, preferably from international publications on things that are of little or peripheral interest to the catchment. Like Brazil going right wing or the repercussions of Brexit on Lebanese eateries in London. Do not add your agreement or disagreement with any of these posts. Merely say, 'interesting perspective' or 'an off-centre take on something that has been preoccupying me for a bit' or 'this does raise some interesting points'. 'Interesting' is a word that doesn't need you to commit to an ideology or point of view; it doesn't need you to commit to anything at all. For instance, you could say Jack the Ripper was an interesting guy and it doesn't make you a murderous sociopath sympathizer. Use 'interesting' liberally. What does this achieve? Well, it doesn't make you an interesting person for sure. But we *don't* want to attract interest or attention. It gives the impression of a well-read person, and nobody wants to engage with a well-read person on social media. It isn't any fun. So they will leave you to your devices and give you the mind space to check out their photographs freely. Check out photos, stalk updates, but try to be invisible. Comment only occasionally and 'like' infrequently. In the comments section, be pithy and lace your comments with self-pity. 'I envy how you can take time out for a vacation. I have just been so snowed under with work' or 'Great photos. I am living vicariously. Any time I get, I just want to curl up and sleep'.

You see what you are doing there? You are constantly monitoring the social media feed of your friends circle, but they think you are a hyper-productive person who has no time offline or online.

The Supreme Sacrifice

What I am now going to ask you to do will require a supreme sacrifice. This could potentially be the biggest sacrifice that reading this book entails. This is your chance to back out. If you are still reading, though, here is what you have to do. Do not tell people on social media what you eat every day—no daily lunch-hour updates. I know that felt like a physical blow right in the gut; right now, you are gasping for air and your knees feel like jelly. Your eyes are scanning this paragraph and doing a frantic reread; this can't be right, you are telling yourself. I will repeat myself, then, so there is no ambiguity. Do not post details of your lunch online.

Now that you are calmer, reflect quietly. No productive person values their lunch hour. A truly productive person is one who strategically schedules meetings that eat into lunch hour or one who proposes a working lunch. If you have the time to post photos online of your lunch, you have the time to eat lunch, which can only mean you are shirking something that could potentially alter the course of humanity—such as working on an Excel sheet with details of how many cups of coffee team members have in a day and correlating it to performance. Don't do it. Use every minute of your lunch hour to eat lunch, use your entire day to eat lunch, but don't document it. No one needs to know. Let it be a secret you take to your grave. Or take photos if you must, but keep them in a safe and bequeath them to your future generations. Fat good they will do them, but at least you will die happy.

Spectator Sport

You don't need to actually play a sport to enjoy it. We are a nation of a billion people, but only eleven of us actually play cricket for the country. Active participation has nothing to do with intensity of involvement. Treat social media like a spectator sport. Part of the reason why we love being on social media is because there is always a high probability that there is a fight going on somewhere. Divergent opinions clash, people get snarky and snappy, and all of this can get the adrenaline going. But here's the thing: you don't need to be an active participant because:

1. that gives you visibility, which we don't want; and
2. it is finally work, which we absolutely don't want.

But being passive doesn't mean you don't do anything. You can still be in a state of active passivity. I will demonstrate how.

Friend A posts a status update on how a vegan diet is benefiting her—an innocuous enough update. Here is how you can set off a fire without even lighting a matchstick. Follow instructions carefully.

Friend A: Feeling healthy. My new vegan diet, which is purely plant-based, is just what I needed to sort myself out.

You: That is GRRREAT! You are looking so good too. @FriendB says you need animal protein, but to each their own. Both of you look so good following your individual preferences; I am so envious. I have no time to even think about my diet.

Friend B: You are so going to compromise on your immunity. You need protein to build muscle. There is no B12 in a plant-based diet. I would strongly recommend you go for a balanced diet with at least eggs.

Friend A: Hey. Thanks. But I'm good. You can get B12 from tofu and soya so I think that's sorted. But thanks for your input. Appreciate it!

(This is when you step in again because it is all too cordial, but your expert eye can detect undercurrents. Rise to the occasion.)

You: That's sorted then, one man's tofu is another man's steak. It's a question of preference as long as nobody is forcing their diet on anyone else. Okay. Going for a meeting now.

(You know people turning into vegetarian prigs is a sore point with Friend B, a rabid carnivore, and this is how you segue the conversation by introducing the element of coercion. Your meeting, of course, doesn't exist.)

Friend B: The problem is that the vegetarian mafia is taking the moral high ground and shaming people on their food choices. I mean, well done with your tandoori tofu but give me a tandoori chicken any day.

Friend A: I don't remember forcing my food choices on you. I prefer not to eat chicken, which is full of antibiotics. And talking about vegetarian mafia, at least I don't vote for a political party that interferes with what people have on their plates.

(You have selected well: Friend A is a left liberal and Friend B is mildly right wing; when he orders chicken wings, he almost always eats the right one.)

Friend B: I didn't call you the vegetarian mafia, but clearly it hit home. If you have such a problem with India, why don't you go to liberal Pakistan? I am sure they will have a lot of vegan options there. Or like most commie hypocrites, you will go and eat beef kebabs there to show how liberal you are.

Friend A: I am not going anywhere. This is as much my country as it is yours. Stop wasting my time. Go save a cow or something.

Friend B: I will book your tickets to Rawalpindi. See if your liberal Pakistan lets you eat pork. Nobody minds violating the sentiments of Hindus, because we don't hit back.

Friend A: What makes you more Hindu than I am? Who has given you the right to speak for all Hindus?

(At this deliciously poised juncture, you will step back in. With some luck, others have joined the conversation and the battle lines have been drawn.)

You: Guys. What just happened? I just got off my con call and I need to rush into another meeting. I just want to say peace, guys. Live and let live. There is no need for such toxicity. I am exiting this conversation. Let's be grown-up about this.

(You can now allow yourself a cackle of pure glee. You will be ignored—and you want to be ignored. But for the record, your distressed protest will stay. You can now spend the rest of the morning monitoring this thread as more people join in and Friend A and B block each other. That also gives you enough ammunition: screenshots that you can send to other friends expressing your shock at how things came to such an unfortunate pass.)

To reinforce the point: you don't need to actually play a sport to enjoy it. Always be a smart spectator.

A Conscience

A conscience is a good thing to have on social media. Display it. Be woke. You don't actually need to do anything except sign a lot of online petitions. Aim for at least one petition per month. All it takes for you to be a crusader for gender equality, LGBT rights or farmers' rights is one tweet or one post. Sometimes, you might need to stretch yourself a bit more; you might need to change the filter on your display photo. It might take slightly more effort than you bargained for, but do it. Nobody will begrudge you your hyperactive conscience. Nobody will for a minute suspect that it might be because you have a lot of time on your hands. A few discerning friends might catch on to your slacktivism (google it), but the trick is not to have discerning friends. A good pre-emptive strike: write a post on slacktivism and how it is the bane of this generation. I would have, but I am occupied with an online petition on how people who don't get their kids vaccinated against rubella are making it dangerous for other kids. It is just criminally callous. I don't have kids, but why should that stop anyone.

Cherry-Pick What You Post

Now that we have decided that you cannot be indiscriminate in what you post on social media, a quick recap—don't do food, do vacations sparingly (and if you must, make sure to mention how your family had to keep you away from work emails and updates) and don't do social outings. You can actually do all of these, of course, but don't post about them on social media. You cannot be seen as having a work–life balance. However, what you can do to create the façade of productivity is to post work updates. This is your opportunity to slip in the odd photo or two—chronicle meetings, business trips, offsites, the random coffee, the Uber ride to the office on a rainy day. This gives you the opportunity to invest in a chic work wardrobe (for the photographs) and you can also try out Photoshop/filters without a qualm. Here are some examples of how you can work this.

Example 1
Photo: You in the conference room. Make sure to catch that solitary ray of sunlight right on your face. A coffee mug in front of you. Take as many attempts as needed to get this photo right. It isn't like you're doing anything else anyway.

Post: What is a good three-hour brainstorm without a little bit of caffeine? So chuffed with the ideas that the team came up with. And exhausted (but work is my adrenalin).

Example 2
Photo: You are in a random city for a random meeting, which could have been done via a video call. But why reduce carbon emissions from air travel if you have a choice? First, of course, do the check-in into the city in question on Facebook, and then post a photo of yourself in an eatery eating biryani.

Post: Rushed one-day trip to Hyderabad. Packed schedule; supercharged but hey, a man's got to eat! And it is the biryani capital of India where I have been fortunate enough to set up our new office and directly supervise a team of fifteen enthusiastic Hyderabadis. Love the city. Love the vibe. Will be back soon! Work is Worship.

Motivational Quotes

Now this is really low-hanging fruit, but if you are without a single original thought in your head and yet want to register presence on social media, this could be your way out. Don't share funny memes; let all of your graphics-led posts be motivational and inspirational—they are your morning pep talk to yourself, your arsenal to take on a challenging workday. They also suggest the high levels of stress that you are combating bravely and taking on the chin one motivational quote at a time. You are bound to get approving reactions from other social media warriors as they too jump in to combat the many travails of clashing conference calls. All of this goes a long way in creating a constant buzz around your social media persona.

In conclusion, being active on social media can work out perfectly for the status quo-ist; and the best thing you can do for yourself is to start believing in the illusion of productivity that you have created.

Believe in your lie—when you do that, it is no longer a lie.

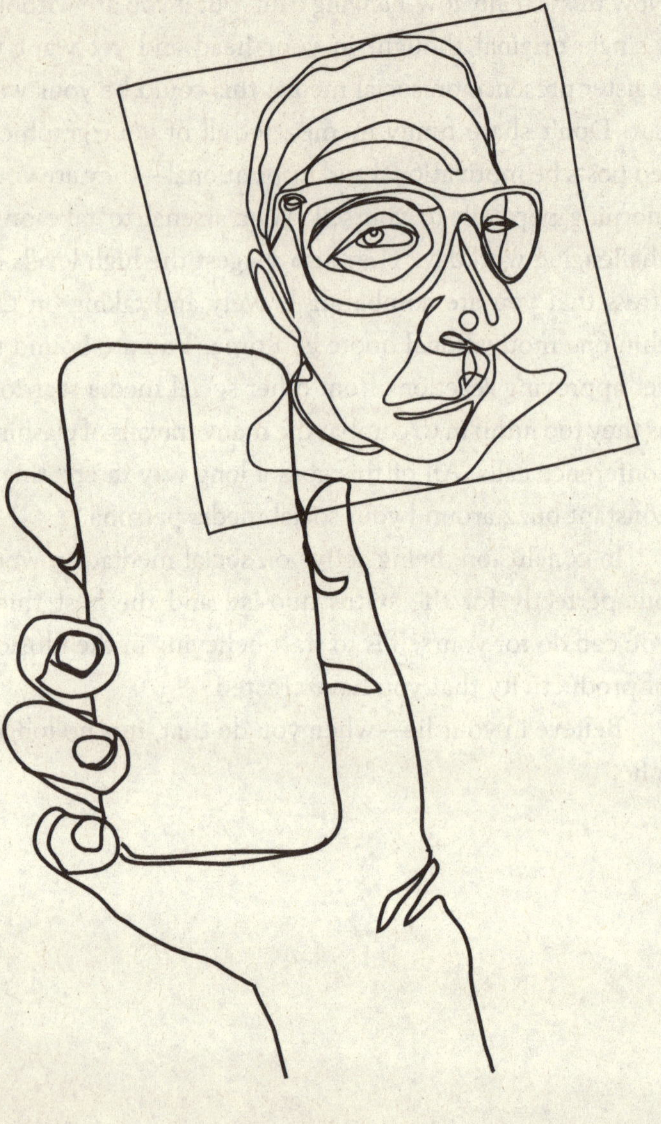

4

How to Be a Gainfully Occupied Freeloader

Once upon a time, a vacation was a once-in-a-year ritual. It coincided with school holidays, and people bundled themselves off to a relative's place in a bigger city or a smaller town. They didn't stay in hotels or eat in exotic restaurants. They took very few photos—most of which were of relatives standing in a line and gawking at the camera. The early edition camera could not make phone calls or send texts and was a severely limited gadget. And then just like that, the holiday would end in a pleasant blur and your forebears were back to negotiating domesticity in their own space. One vacation morphed into the other, a haze of dull sameness—like all lives in the pre-Internet era.

Then 1991 and liberalization happened and your ancestors realized the joys of a minor wardrobe tweak: deeper pockets. And gradually, the annual holiday was not just about visiting relatives. It wasn't even annual any more; it was a lot more frequent. Train travel gave way to air travel. Homes gave way to hotels and there was even the foreign-vacation-package traveller. Descendants of the early Indian traveller soon started topping lists of the worst dressed and worst behaved tourists in the world. So far, they were still paying for their holidays. And a holiday was something they did when they took time off from work. They treated it like an indulgence.

This trip into time might leave you feeling a tad disoriented—and not just because we are not a culture that values history. Like me, you must wonder how we are descendants of people with such limited powers of imagination and productive ability. And then, you must wonder at how evolution got its act together so fast. Today, the human race has worked itself to an enviable position where there is no distinction between work and holiday. In fact, you can get paid to be on holiday. Other people can work and pay for your holiday—and they are not your parents or spouse or the elusive dying spinster aunt who will bequeath you her millions. They are not even your friends.

Unrelated tip: don't borrow money from friends if you can help it. It stresses out the friendship. Try and swindle strangers instead. There is very little emotional baggage there.

So how do you get other people to pay for your holidays? First, it is very 1991 to call them holidays, so don't. Call them 'explorations' or 'journeys' and you have immediately imbued your trip with meaning and a larger philosophical purpose. Then let the journey have a purpose; it's a bit like Miss India. The goal is never a Bollywood film debut. It is world peace; a career in the movies is just a byproduct. Similarly, your 'journey' has no recreational purpose: it is something you are doing to test yourself and challenge your limits—and the world owes you that chance. Yes, you heard right. You clear your dues to yourself, but the world picks up the tab.

Let me reproduce almost verbatim a conversation I had with a young enlightened person (Yeppie) a few years back.

Yeppie: I am so done with my job and the rat race. I am taking a sabbatical. Taking off.

Me: You're going on a holiday? A vacation will be good for you. Come back recharged. Why quit though?

Take the month off. Eat some good food. Chill and you'll be as good as new.

Yeppie: I am not going on a vacation. I am taking the year off; I will be visiting thirty countries and the challenge is to learn one new thing in every country. This will help people and countries come together. I will blog about it, and I will come out of the journey with an expanded outlook. I need to do this for myself and for the world.

Me: You have enough savings for this? Your bank balance will be exhausted.

Yeppie: I have started a crowdfunding campaign. I am asking people to participate in my journey. To join me as I find myself.

Me: So it's like a group package tour?

Yeppie: No. They won't physically come with me. They will discover themselves as I discover myself. They will live the journey through my blog and Instagram feed.

Me: So they will pay for a holiday that they won't go on. What sort of idiots are these? And you're okay with begging strangers for money to go on a holiday?

Yeppie (frostily): It's crowdfunding—an initiative that helps people in these troubled times to come together. To say that in spite of our differences, the kernel of humanity that binds us is the same. It is a salve for toxicity. It would be great if you could help this cause.

Me: My contribution to your journey will pretty much be what my presence on your journey will be: only in spirit.

Needless to say, the tenuous relationship between Yeppie and I ended at that point. I take full responsibility: I was far too much of a skinflint. Luckily for her, not everyone was that mean-spirited. She did embark on her crowdfunded expedition and has managed ten-odd countries. However, her journey hasn't yet translated into a Nobel Peace Prize or her learning any skill worth mentioning—which is truly baffling. But one birdbrain does not a summer make, and therefore we owe it to her to amplify her movement and come up with other lofty journeys to save humanity. Never mind the carbon emissions the world will have to deal with because of frequent air travel; it is collateral damage to finally save it. There may not be anything left to save, but notionally we will save it. It is the thought that counts.

Here are some ideas for crowdfunded vacays, sorry, explorations that you can go for:

1. An expedition to the United Kingdom to shake off your colonial hangover. You stand on the banks of the Thames and expunge the ghosts of our collective past on a FB live stream.
2. Couch-surfing through South America. Sixty days, thirty couches—what does that do for your understanding of race, and bedbugs? Technical question: Is it still a bedbug if it is on a couch?
3. Top thirty Bollywood destinations. Visit thirty destinations that meant varied things at different

difficult points of time to you. Ask people to crowdfund your catharsis because the world owes you your sense of well-being and mental health.

4. Or you could try honesty—just call it the entitled millennial trip. Here is your pitch: I was fortunate enough to be born in a generation where my parents have pretty much figured out the major stuff like house, car, food. I need an existential crisis to make my rather comfortable life exciting. Don't stress about that, I am good at conjuring up frequent bouts of unprovoked angst. I also know that travelling the world will help soften the blow of getting things far too easily. But I am woke and will not ask my parents to pay for anything beyond clothing and feeding me. However, I am also broke, so I expect you to help alleviate my angst with a contribution to my self-exploration. Wire transfers will do. Let's save paper and not write out cheques. Small gestures to save the environment.

Now all you need to do is get a little bit of buzz around your journey. Put your pitch up as an interestingly written Instagram or FB post. Be careful how you phrase it, though.

Example: Photo of you peering intently into the camera. Try a black and white filter.

Caption: There is a story inside all of us. My story cries out to be told; dealing with a Victorian-style convent education has colonized my soul. As I shake off the external trappings, I know the fix is internal. I am going for #ThePurge. My ancestors went to the Ganges to cleanse their souls. I am going to the Thames and that is where I will wash off for our country centuries of inadequacy and colonization. Let's do this for our ancestors; every rupee counts. You can write me a cheque or you can Paytm me. #ThePurge

A young intern at a media house whose job is to scour the Internet will be suitably impressed and will write a listicle on Why Millennials Don't Want a Ganga Snaan But Are Headed to the Thames Instead. This will generate fodder for many more listicles and social media chatter. Other articles on you could be:

1. Thames Up for Western Civilization: Why Young India Is Snubbing the Colonial Legacy
2. The Great Indian Millennial Purge: Five Reasons Why We Think It Is Lit
3. You Will Never Believe Why This Millennial Wants to Go to the Thames. Our Jaws Dropped . . .
4. Move Over Ganges, Thames Is the Purge You Need
5. As More and More Urban Indians Are Saffronized, a Reverse Racism Takes Root in Millennials. Are These the Early Signs of a Theocratic State?
6. The Right Wing and Its Sinister Reverse Indoctrination

With this kind of buzz around your trip, rest assured there will be enough people out there to pick up the tab. With some luck, you might even fly premium economy.

There is an even easier way to get people to pay for your vacations, and you don't need to link it to either your conscience, a cause, or your Aadhar card. Become an influencer—not on Facebook, not on Twitter, but on Instagram. A Twitter influencer can be any or all of these: opinionated, well-read, a curator of other opinions, funny, rabid, liberal, right wing, moderate, erudite, ignorant. You need to engage, bait, provoke and inform. All of this for free, nobody pays you. An Instagram influencer just needs to have a good camera phone. You need to post photos—with hashtags. Banality is highly recommended. You can get paid to do this or you can get a host of freebies. It is all par for the course.

Your followers on Twitter judge you if you try to monetize your tweets; you are a sell-out if you do brand collaborations or paid partnerships. They follow you for your thoughts. You have to be above paying your bills. Simple Living, High Thinking. On Twitter, the most you would get is a free movie ticket, if you are lucky. The best way, then, to a life of gainful freeloading is Instagram, except you don't call it freeloading. You call it a collaboration: your followers for their freebies. It is a fair deal.

So how do you crack being an Instagram celebrity and how do you get people to follow you? You could try being famous like a movie star, a cricketer or a chef. But that involves effort—acting school, cricket coaching, some kind of basic skill set, which if you had, you wouldn't be reading this book. This is a book about minimum effort and least resistance. Hard-fought-for fame is not part of our plan. However, Instagram is a great platform to give you the fame of singular non-achievement.

But even in the field of non-achievement, the key is not to aspire for great heights. This is not a chapter for Kylie Jenner (it has been variously reported that she charges a million dollars for one post). We don't want that staggering level of non-achievement fame. Moderation, as I have said ad nauseam, is what we strive for. What we want are the crumbs: the occasional free meal, discounts and maybe the odd junket—nothing too high profile. The aim is to make you a micro-influencer. You have a following in the thousands, you don't have an agent and you would do a post for a free coffee. Let's set the bar low and be realistic. Here is a quick guide to a life of freebies and deals for the micro-influencer:

1. Photograph everything. Invest in a good camera phone and shoot everything. If you are a woman, most of your followers will be quite happy if you post a 'Good Morning' selfie every day. But don't do this as a vanity exercise. Be sure to write a few words of inspiration.
    Example: The visual is of you peering into the camera with a hint of a smile. Don't wear too much make-up. Use a filter to give you that dewy fresh look.
    Caption: Another morning is another chance to live the day. This time I will do it right. Or maybe, I won't. But I know I will do it my way. Good Morning. #Blessed #LoveMyLife #MorningPerson

2. Stock up on Rumi and Kahlil Gibran. You don't always have to be penning your own motivational quotes. Luckily for us, Rumi, Gibran and many other great writers, anticipating Instagram, have left us a handy bank of quotes that can be used for anything. Your pet cat, your cup of coffee, the stray pimple on your nose and even your garbage bags with dry and wet separated. Example: The visual is of the stray pimple on your nose. Frankly, it is rather unsightly, but here is how you can use it to your advantage on Instagram. Use a filter so the pimple looks like a little blob of luminosity instead of the monstrosity it is.

   Caption: I woke up to this pimple. It disturbed me. I wanted to hide away, but then I remembered.

   'If you are irritated by every rub, how will your mirror be polished?'—Rumi

   And so here I am—warts and all. Facing up to you. Facing up to the mirror. This is my reality. I face it. Embrace your fears. #NoFilters #LoveYourself #LoveYourPimple

3. TMI. There is no concept of TMI—too much information—on Instagram. Instagram is about NTMI—never too much information. You are expected to chronicle every moment of your waking life. Tell your followers what you eat, drink and think. The more real you seem, the more traction you get. It has to look honest and organic, even if it isn't really. Create stories about yourself. You don't have

to be particularly insightful—just prolific. There is no such thing as oversharing. Also, from time to time, bung in the #warrior. People like to be thought of as warriors even if they are just drinking sugarless coffee or having a daily shower.

Example: Visual of coffee cup. You could be holding it. Caption: Three days without sugar. Next: get rid of the milk. The battle is real. #Warrior #IWillSurvive #IronWill

4. Relevance and utility. While this is a book that encourages you to be generally useless, you have to aspire to have some kind of utility on Instagram to build a following. Find your area of interest: travel, beauty, make-up, fitness, fashion or food. These are all fairly simple things to be interested in, and apart from fitness, require little or no effort. Become a master of a no-effort skill and demonstrate to your following the effort it needs. This will help get you the volumes, and the freebies will follow.

As Rumi said, 'Let yourself be drawn by the stronger pull of that which you truly love.'

The quote is actually completely irrelevant here, but because it sounds profound, you didn't even notice how misplaced it was. Or maybe it wasn't misplaced: the 'stronger pull' could be the freeloading you so desire and aspire to. Let that then guide you, and the life of gainful freeloading is just one social media post away.

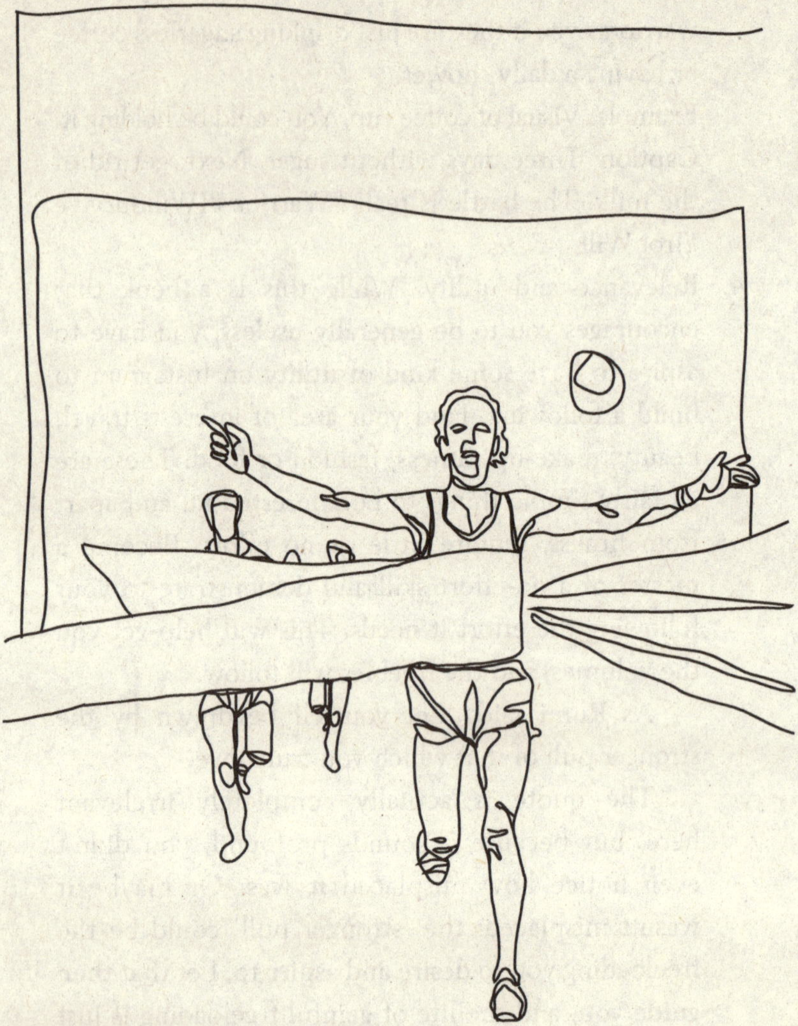

5

How to Be Unfit and Be Morally Superior OR How to Be Fit and Not Invite Resentment

There is fit, and then there IS fit. There is a kind of fitness that doesn't bother people. It is a state that is remote and inaccessible—the preserve of happy, shiny, yet shadowy people who we are not likely to ever meet, such as movie stars or sportspeople or models. These are people whose occupational hazard is looking a certain way. These are not people like us, and as we imagine the army of trainers and dieticians that makes them look the way they do, there is much to seek self-righteous comfort in. We don't have the luxury of fitness. We have to work hard to pay our bills and manage our daily commute and deal with our snotty brats. The rich and the famous are born with the karmic good fortune of walking a path that is actually a treadmill. In our next lives, we will be fitter. But in this lifetime, it is not in our fate. Pass those French fries as we ruminate deeply.

But then something deeply disturbing happens: your neighbour starts yoga, your colleague runs five kilometres every day before coming in to work and your plump school friend is now a Pilates enthusiast and is displaying visible abs. There is a contagion. Half your friends circle is now training for the marathon. It is a crisis; you frantically try to pass off your half-hour dawdle around the building compound as a structured exercise regimen, but you are only leading yourself up the garden path. You try to race away from the truth. You break into a cold sweat, but it catches up with you. If these ordinary blokes can, why can't you? They too come preloaded with bills, commute woes and bad karma.

There is no easy way to understand human deviance, and this is not the book for it. This is a book about easy answers. We don't seek complexity. We seek complacency, and this is how we will achieve it.

Here is what you can do to win the battle over fitness, to assure yourself and others that while the path you have chosen may not burn any calories, it is morally superior. Calories can be empty, but never your conscience. There are a few approaches to waging this battle, which I will briefly elaborate upon. All of them will lead you to a moral high ground.

Guilt-Tripping

As they break into a canter, all you need to stop them in their stride is to trip them—literally and figuratively. Furtively sneak in guilt. Make them apologetic about having the time to have a routine that involves exercise.

They are clearly slacking off work or leaving their children in the care of negligent nannies or are just plain vain. Be appreciative of their effort but always have an undertone that hints at a grave dereliction of a larger duty. You don't need to define what that duty is—just that it is being criminally overlooked. Never let them bandy the view that the pursuit of fitness is a duty too. It is at best an indulgence and at worst, vanity. Make them uneasy and apologetic, leading them to treat fitness like a guilty pleasure. This will stop them from flaunting it. It is their dark secret, which they will take to their graves. And once we are all dead, how does it matter if our tummies were not equally toned?

An Affliction

Convince the world that this breed of marathoners, yoga practitioners and weightlifters has an affliction, that their moderate activity is some kind of extreme adventure sport—one that will maim them for sure and might even kill them. There will always be the odd case of a cardiac arrest in the gym or during a marathon. Highlight those cases, especially of that one friend who monitored every calorie he consumed but had three blockages in his heart. Or that one freak case who did headstands every day and then died of a brain aneurysm. Cluck now in sympathy as you watch your neighbour, armed with her yoga mat, trudge to a certain death. There is enough empirical evidence based purely on the study of stray anecdotes that suggests that something indefinable is propelling these individuals along the path of self-destruction. You need to show this up. If you can portray the mildly fit to be the mildly suicidal, your work on this planet is done. You need to remove the aspiration value from the pursuit of fitness and make it about people who are in crisis mode. There are studies out there that suggest that people over thirty-five who are suddenly interested in being fit are dealing with a midlife crisis. They are grappling with a life that is jaded and needs strategic bursts of adrenaline—unlike your sated, comfortable life. There is a difference between being sated and jaded; we aspire for the former. As for the young who seek to be fit, the motivations of the youth in every generation have eluded comprehension and defy rational behaviour so we needn't dwell on them.

In short, you no longer need to resent or envy those people who live their lives measured out in Fitbit numbers. They need only your pity.

Pre-emptive Shaming

This is psychological warfare and could be a tad problematic. There are some perfectly horrible people who bully overweight people. Fat-shaming is an odious thing. But not everyone who follows a healthy diet or goes to the gym thrice a week is a fat-shamer. However, you can lead them into believing they are: you need to throw words such as 'body positivity' and 'body dysmorphic disorder' at them. Make them feel that by doing what they are, they are being disrespectful to people who can't lose weight for a variety of medical or psychological reasons. Here is the thing: they are welcome to be fit; we just don't want to see them pass it off as the new normal. Let them maintain a respectful silence, and we will mind our own business. The strategy is pre-emptive strikes: before they tell you, you tell them. Tell them about eating disorders, about the exploitative beauty industry, about hypothyroidism, about morbid obesity and watch them skulk away. Watch them on their walk of shame. You then proceed to amble along in a haze of righteousness. Now for the second part of our exercise.

The above might have given some of you the mistaken notion that the status quo-ist and the complacent will necessarily be a couch potato. Not true: one size doesn't fit all. Complacence is inclusive. It welcomes diversity. You could pursue fitness, but your mindset could be that of a potato. The spirit is unwilling, the body is not. Our goal is that you behave like a potato; whether you look like one is incidental. In fact, we encourage you to be fixated on a physically exacting regimen, which will help keep your mind comfortably empty.

But how do you do all this and yet not draw attention to yourself? There are Type A personalities who are fitness fiends, but they are attention junkies, while you, on the other hand, are mildly apologetic about your existence. Your pursuit of fitness must be an unobtrusive one—one that invites neither resentment nor rancour, but lets you discreetly fit into the size you want without anyone itching to cut you down to size.

Here is how you can achieve the above.

1. Don't be a fitness evangelist
   Yes. Yoga sorted out your breathing. Going off gluten sorted out your gut. You can dead lift fifty kilos. Good for you. Nobody needs to know. Let it be your deep dark secret. You don't need to change how the world, your colleagues or your family live unless it is your job and you are getting paid to do so. Admit only to the occasional walk. This also means no fitness-related social media updates. Don't panic, though: there are exceptions.

2. If you must run, let it only be the marathon
   The one thing you can and should flaunt is running marathons. In the corporate world, running a marathon fits in well with workforce culture. It doesn't seem like a vanity project, and it always sounds like it has a larger purpose. It is the kind of thing that management approves of—chugging along for hours at a stretch guided by a lofty goal, which you don't have a clue about. It is like your work life: it is relentless; it taxes you; it can be deathly boring, but you stay the course till you reach your objective.

If you are willing to run a marathon, you are willing to be a workhorse. It is subliminal. Now you know. Get those sneakers on.

3. Align fitness to a larger cause; bore people
   Never be fit in a vacuum. I cannot begin to describe how badly that will go against you. If you must post updates about your regimen, make sure to have profound messaging attached to them. Make it about exploring the inward tranquillity of humanity, restoring the balance of nature and freeing your inner demons. Write long, verbose posts on these; nobody will read them but nobody will grudge you your regimen either. You are a tormented soul, battling yourself, and all you will get is sympathy. While the rest of us can be smug and happy that such searing existential dilemmas have eluded us. Always bore people; you stop being a threat.

The above, then, are the broad guidelines you need to follow, irrespective of the type of couch potato you aim to be.

Now we move on from the rather cozy world of office battles to a more sinister, treacherous terrain. This one will need a lot of work. And we might need to abandon all hitherto known battle strategies and go back to the drawing board.

We move on to our most perilous frontier yet: Mummy Politics.

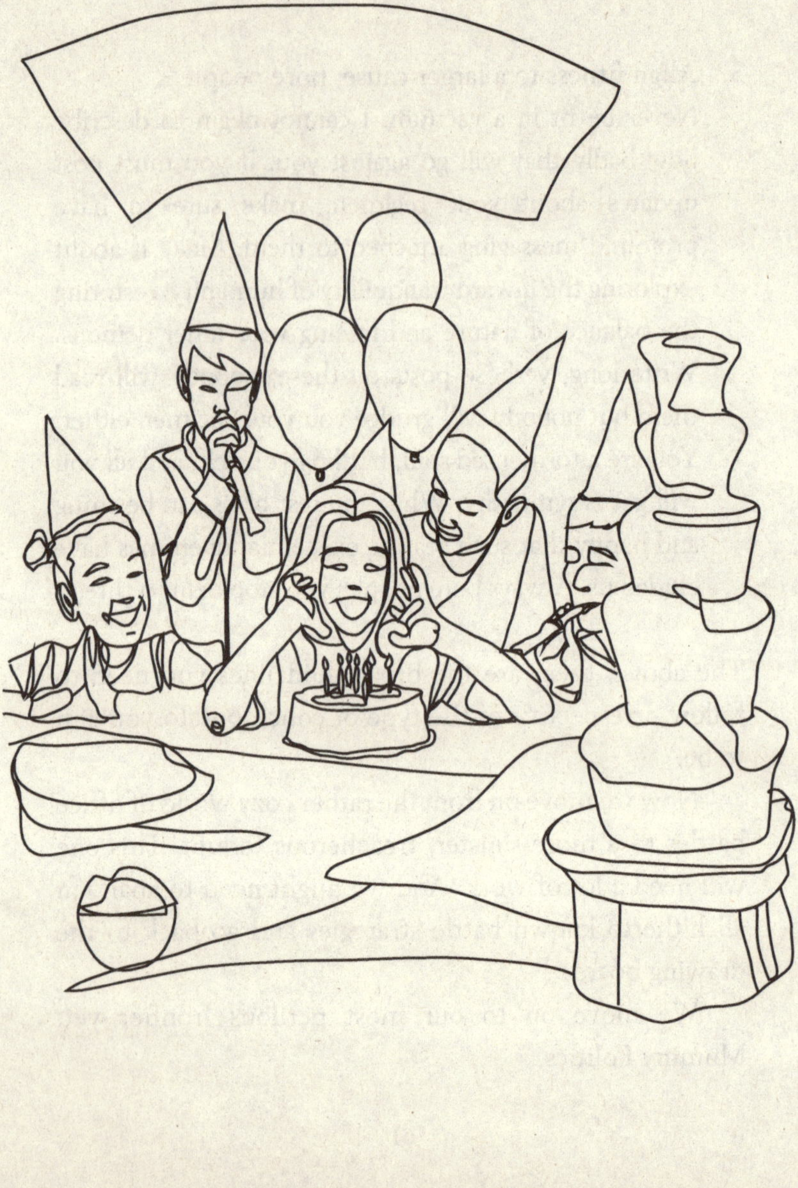

6

Mummy Politics for the Dummy

If you are a woman, the toughest thing you will do is become a mummy. I don't mean the process of childbirth and the inordinate time it takes to carry the baby to term. That is the easy part. That is the motherhood part of the deal—the subject of many sappy Hallmark cards, not the subject of this book.

This is about the time you are officially ordained a 'mummy'. And this usually happens when you become part of a 'mums only' WhatsApp group. This isn't any other group. This is turf that will test your mettle in ways you didn't think possible. One day, you can aspire to be Administrator of the group; but to begin with, take it slow.

There is an entire generation of mums out there who reared their children without being on WhatsApp groups. Needless to say, their parenting methods were deficient. Your initiation into a mums' WhatsApp group will begin when your child hits five. You could do a trial run with playschool groups, but that is not the real thing. Five is a crucial year: it marks the passage from toddler to adulting. It is the year when your child starts reading, writing, talking in complete sentences—pretty much all the qualifications he or she will ever need in the adult world. Everything else is a superfluous add-on. These are also milestones that can be competitive and comparative, and will give enough fodder for edgy WhatsApp conversations.

It takes an incredibly selfish mum to opt out of WhatsApp groups. It could mean your child misses out on birthday parties and is on the way to social maladjustment. You see, if your child is not attending a birthday party every weekend, you are doing something terribly wrong—but more on birthday parties later. Let's first get you to survive the murky world of the WhatsApp group.

It starts innocuously enough: one morning, you will wake to find that you are now part of a group called *Insert School Name* Mums. It is all quite cheerful in the beginning—just a bunch of regular, pleasant-sounding mums journeying along with you on this life experience called motherhood. That is the brochure. And you know what lies beneath a brochure: the truth. Crack the surface, and it is a minefield of insecurity, hyper-competition, upmanship and fragile self-worth. These are the various kinds of mums that you could potentially meet and each of them will require a customized approach that I will, of course, help you with.

Alpha Stay-at-Home Capitalist Mum

She may or may not have had a job before she became a mum. Right now, she is an exemplar of involved motherhood. She is usually the Administrator of the group. She is also the moving force behind play dates, which can't be what their names suggest they are—dates where you simply play. They are exercises to build development and personality skills—hone the mental faculties of the child. Each play date must have a thematic larger purpose. This is the mum whom you must endear yourself to—she will always know everything there is to know about not just her child, but your child too. This mother is a willing victim of the forces of consumerism: she often judges education by how much she pays for it. She is also the voice of censure and moral authority in the group. She is unsparing and non-selective in her judgement of maternal lapses. For all her foibles, this mum is straightforward: what you see is what you get. You would be well advised to be a crony to this capitalist.

Guilt-Tripping Tiger Mum

This is the mum trying to balance a career with the demands of a WhatsApp group; the parenting part is easy to juggle. She lives in fear that she will be judged and her game is the catch-up game. You can count on her to overspend on birthdays. It is her way of compensating. She is at the receiving end of most of the capitalist mum's censure. You can cast yourself as her confidante with generous oodles of empathy.

Creative Hipster Mum

This is the mum who probably runs a yoga studio as a part-time career. Her chakras are aligned and she doesn't really fret the small stuff like paying bills. Investment banker husband does that. She is about Zen and deep breathing, and she radiates peace. The other mums can't bring themselves to resent her as they are slightly intimidated by her in-your-face unworldliness. Her child often makes it to her Instagram stories, almost like a substitute for a yoga block. Her presence on the group is wraith-like: she wafts in and out, only displaying aggression when it comes to hard-selling her yoga classes. This mum you can be friendly with, but don't seek too much intimacy as she can be flaky.

Strident Socialist Mum

This is a complicated personality type. This is actually an alpha consumerist mum in disguise. She has all the advantages of a capitalistic set-up—a domestic workforce, IB schools, MNC jobs, club membership—but her soul is socialist. She likes to believe that her child-rearing methods have more meaning. She occasionally shares that she might just homeschool her children, throws eco-friendly birthday parties and gives plants as return gifts. She is always slightly superior—as if she has transcended the material world even as she soaks in every conceivable material comfort. She doesn't moralize; she evangelizes. There is a difference. She is also the mum who will occasionally forward the woke article on 'How We Should Let Our Child Get Bored', which you can pretend not to notice. You can alternate between being besties with her and the alpha consumerist mum. Remember to brush up on your Vedic maths; it is the kind of thing she will approve of.

You

Which brings us to you. Since this is a book that encourages being vanilla and bland as the best self-preservation techniques for the human race, you know what you have to do. Actually, you don't have a clue, do you? When in doubt, insert an emoticon. You must have received this forward (usually on WhatsApp) on how God couldn't be everywhere, so he created mums. Awww, ya. That cheesy PR spiel of motherhood. I have a slight revision to that for WhatsApp groups. When mums can't be everywhere, they insert emoticons. Let most of your communication be via emoticons, and even when you have a wide array to choose from, be restrained. Restrict yourself to the non-committal cautious smile and the occasional clap. This way, nobody really notices you and nobody then competes with you, talks you down or resents you. The human need to stand up and be counted will finally lead to its annihilation. Play the WhatsApp game well and you could be the last survivor in an apocalypse film.

While I have kept the rules of engagement specific to mummy groups, this approach can be tweaked to guide you through the travails and turbulence of many such groups:

1. Housing society group. Usually a collection of mildly murderous men and rabid conspiracy theorists. Might also raise the bar occasionally and fit in the fully fledged psychopath who could plot mass murder if denied a building Holi party.
2. Yoga group. A haze of benign competition and one where you will not be judged by your ability to think on your feet. Quite the contrary—you will be judged on your headstand. You didn't see that coming, did you?
3. Work groups. A black hole of grandstanding. But you get paid for this. Go forth and unleash those emoticons. This we have already covered extensively.
4. School group. This is the vague memories group and you stay on for reasons of vague nostalgia. Stay vague and you should do well here as well.

After that slight diversion, let us return to negotiating the state of parenthood. The phase between five and twelve is crucial in your child's life. Of course, these are the formative years—the years when you hope your rather ordinary gene pool has miraculously mutated to produce a super-achiever child. But once you reluctantly let go of that hopeful delusion, you will realize that these years are singularly important because it is in this phase that you will face your biggest parenting challenge: the birthday party.

There was a time when India was either poor or lower middle-class. This was the time we grew up in. Our birthday parties had cake and wafers on paper plates; we had orange squash and we dutifully played musical chairs. Return gifts were scented erasers. It was the universal middle-class homogenized experience, which produced middle-class homogenized offspring.

Then India changed: it still remained largely poor, but the middle class suddenly had money. A heady mix of aspiration and affluence led to bigger cars, bigger flats, foreign holidays, club memberships, an IB school education for the kids and the birthday party. The birthday party for your child became a symbol of your achievement. The middle-class homogenized person who now could have everything bespoke and customized. For his or her bespoke, customized child.

There is no limit to what birthday parties can set out to do—superhero theme parties with iPads as return gifts, pool parties, parties in amusement parks and parties in beach bungalows with a three-foot chocolate fountain. Mums spend months planning these events and the bad news is that you can't opt out. In this one case, I cannot advise passivity. Here, you have to keep up with the Joneses, the Shuklas, the Jains, the Singhs, the Rizvis, the Lobos, the Ambanis (the last one perhaps you could skip unless you are an Adani).

So here is the thing: do not try to up the ante on what can be done within the realms of a birthday party. That is not the personality type we are trying to mould you into. You don't compete; you fit in. I am going to present you with a list of the minimum you can do to ensure your child is not a social outcast. Following this list will not make your party stand out, but it won't make it stick out like a sore thumb either.

Here goes then.

1. Plan. Plan. Plan. You should plan for at least six months in advance. Get a fix on the venue, caterers and party game organizers.
2. Theme. No self-respecting child does a non-theme party. Send out invites two months in advance so that objects on display, sorry, the children, can get fitted out in their costumes.
3. Do a party at home only if the theme is retro. And you can only pull this off once.

70

4. You can leave everything to the party organizers, but you will be judged for being an impersonal host. So sign up for cupcake classes and bake cupcakes for the brats, or decorate the venue yourself. Fill the balloons with your personalized breath.

5. The same applies to return gifts. They cannot be generic; each has to be individually tailored to the likes of your attendee children. Please wrap these presents yourself.

6. I am assuming you are affluent if you have read so far down this list because all this is expensive. But if you're not, keep healthy. You never know when you might need to sell off an organ—or two.

7. There is no such thing as too much affluence though. You don't have to be a complete spendthrift. After all, there are still minor things such as the child's education, marriage etc., that you will need to fund even after the twelfth birthday party. This might feel a bit uncomfortable, but seasoned birthday party hosts do this well. They mention explicitly that the party is for the kids and not the parents. How do you do this without sounding like a scrimper? Write 'Nanny Drop Only' on your invites. That usually gets the message across.

   PS: Make sure you have a nanny too

8. This also reduces food expenses as caterers will give you nanny food packages, which are half the price of the regular party food. This might smack of class bias, but don't let that trifle bother you. Focus on the truffle instead. Nannies get to eat the same cake. You are generous that way.

9. If you are wondering why this plan only holds till the twelfth birthday, it's because after that, your child will turn into a teenager. And post that, you will not want to celebrate his or her birth for some time.

The above then will help you set up a forgettable, generic and expensive celebration. While it might not be memorable, it will go down as a pleasant-enough life experience that you will not be judged on, a carefully customized and curated experience that is comforting in its conformity.

We were brought up to be middle class and bland. Our children will be affluent and bland. Bland is good.

The birthday party is of course the most crucial parenting challenge that will be presented to mums. But your job doesn't end with it. Being a mum is managing the administrative aspect of childhood; the logistics are your department. Even the most diligent of husbands finally play the role of senior management in the parenting equation—lots of ideas, but none of which make too much sense (plug for subsequent chapter on kangaroo dads). However, the practical execution of the ideas is your headache.

Here are a few pointers on how not to be a tiger mum—how to compromise on what the world has made you believe is essential for good mothering. You are not slacking off; you are just keeping sane. You are in the race, but you are running at your own pace. You probably won't win a medal, but you will reach the finish line and your kids will be more or less fine. They might even be prodigies, and it won't be because you gave up on everything else besides them. At the very least, they will be average, well-adjusted blobs of generic humanity and not over-entitled, over-indulged misfits. You are doing them a favour—and yourself too. Ease off motherhood.

Here is a step-by-step breakdown on how to be a no-frills mum who coexists with hyper-combative mums and, more importantly, doesn't let them catch on to your laxity.

1. Mute the mummy WhatsApp group. You can't exit. This is not a book that encourages rebellion. It is too much work. However, you can mute notifications and every so often clear media without reading any of the 500 messages you left unread. The other mums are too self-involved to notice your passive participation. Passive participation is the act of inserting emoticons at regular intervals to suggest involvement and engagement.

2. Your child is a potato. Operate on the premise that your little bundle of joy is a regular potato. There is nothing wrong with being a potato. It is essential and versatile. Don't try to turn the potato into an avocado: it is a fad and overrated. It is an acquired taste in any case. A potato, on the other hand, is a lot more wholesome and its ability to blend in cannot be overemphasized. Your potato might show signs of exceptional ability in some cases—at which point, he or she becomes a gifted potato. But a potato nevertheless. Never forget.

3. Acceptance. Accept that between you and your spouse, you are fairly forgettable blobs. And therefore, the chances that you have given birth to a fairly forgettable blob are high. Feed it right, treat it well, educate it and then leave it to its destiny. It isn't possible for your blob to be good in academics, dance, music, gymnastics, writing, badminton, football, swimming, math, nuclear science, coding and international diplomacy all at once. His or her mind doesn't need to be occupied every waking minute; you don't need to plan a class or an activity for the blob 24/7. His or her mind—believe it or not—isn't even that evolved. Give your parenting some breathing space. Give the blob some breathing space. He or she will find their own space.

4. Don't let the world catch on. You have come this far. Congratulations. It is difficult not to be giddy

about your offspring. It is an age-old pull—the bond between a parent and a child. The pride that you feel in your child in a meta way is the pride you feel in yourself. Children are a genetic upgrade, your genetic upgrade. That is why the yank of parenting is emotional and a tad irrational. But now that I have guided you past that stage of self-involved giddiness, one bit of crucial advice: don't let the world catch on. Detached parenthood where you love your child without expectation is not something that is easy to grasp. And what the world doesn't understand, it condemns. Continue, therefore, to go through the rites of overweening parental pride; put up regular updates on how maddeningly cute your child is. The world will concur and if nothing else the likes on your posts will multiply. Chronicle each achievement—from the first time she went on stage to the time he won a consolation prize at the science fair. On the off chance that the child does go on to become a luminary, publishers will be bidding for the memoir rights and your source material will be invaluable.

5. The world is not that into your child. This might be the most bitter pill to swallow, but, well, somebody had to break it to you. Don't ask me why. I don't know. But it just isn't. I know it is inexplicable, but that is the way it is. Your cute baby is interchangeable with other cute babies. People like all cute babies equally. Okay, maybe not. They like Taimur Ali

75

Khan a little bit more. Okay, a lot more than they like your baby. Only you are that into your child. Motherhood makes you believe that a polite interest in your child's well-being means an obsessive need to know everything about the muppet. No. That is never the case. Hold yourself back. Remember the potato principle of child-rearing. Everyone likes potatoes; nobody wants to keep talking about them. This, then, is the final stage of no-frills mummy-hood where you have gone beyond self-awareness to self-actualization.

We don't know whether following any of the above principles will make you a better mummy, but it will definitely make you a more bearable human being. Just for that, give it a shot.

7

How to Be a Kangaroo Dad
(How to Contribute Nothing to Parenting and
Yet Be Dad of the Year)

Few things can be compared to fatherhood—the profound feeling of joy, the elation of seeing the flesh of your flesh, the fruit of your seed, the gleam in your eye, and the wordless demise of your social life.

After the glowing Facebook posts and gushing solidarity from more experienced friends on the all-male WhatsApp group come the more sombre commiserations. Sudden absences at the all-boys poker night are greeted with understanding glances amongst male friends. The presence on the after-work football WhatsApp group becomes one of ghostly, grudging silence. The entry of the newest citizen that the seven-billion-strong planet really needed has meant the cancellation of your passport to the leisurely pursuits of the modern man. The man who once thought he was the king of the jungle, striding across the living room to the door like Prometheus, now sees himself as the male-nanny-in-waiting.

The same hands that once clinked pints of beer deftly, the fingers that scrolled through humorous memes and the mind that internalized the latest Premier League scores are now all engaged in the exciting pursuit of child-rearing. Thrust in the middle of daddy duty are things you never imagined you'd do when you hoped she'd say 'I do!' The holding of breath as you change nappies, the comical gurgling sounds as you try to burp baby, and the sorting of the hapless tangle of small limbs as they waggle about when you are stretching the onesie on.

We have discussed this before, and I reiterate: it is a problematic time to be an urban, modern man. You have to be sensitive and empathetic, and you have to unfortunately contribute more than just your impressive premium-quality sperm. You are now expected to be a hands-on daddy, and even if you don't want to, you have to keep up appearances. Caveat: if you are already an involved, over-invested dad, please go no further with this chapter. This book is for the slacker. If you are the earnest doer dad, there are some great titles on parenting that you should pick up and take your leave now.

Now that we have got that out of the way, let us return to the visual of you trying to change the diaper on the little uncoordinated bundle of humanity you brought into this world. It is at this point that you will begin to notice changes in your otherwise angelic spouse. This is what is happening. You are no longer the centre of her universe. Instead, that flailing, howling, attention-seeking bald drama queen is. Yes. That is how the cookie crumbles into smithereens. Deal with it. Women get obsessive about parenting; this is not a generalization. It is a fact. It is like saying the sky is blue (or murky grey if you live in a big Indian city). And they expect you to share the intensity of the obsession. The expectations of you will accelerate.

Keen to get it right, the love of your life, mother of your child and dutiful wife will turn her gaze sharply on you. Then, with every tiger mom instinct she has, she will train her sights on your abilities and involvement. No longer content to hear you mumble insincere praise of her ability to dilate to superhuman proportions during childbirth, she will demand your engagement in action. Holding you accountable for getting it right just the way her friend's husband does as he assumes the mantle of Daddy of the Year.

These aggressively feline tendencies you will witness in your spouse are already the subject of pop-culture infamy, based on Amy Chua's treatise on what it means to be a tiger mom. It is an illuminating toolbox on terrorizing your children to help them achieve greatness. Titled *The Battle Hymn of the Tiger Mother*, Chua's instruction manual for motherhood expounds on how berating, browbeating and bruising her child's self-esteem will help a mother feel proud about her child's achievements when she meets her friends for dinner. The difference, dear daddy, is that none of this pushy behaviour is ready to be directed towards the angelic lactose-addict with a bowel that has a mind of its own—yet. But, the tiger-mum-in-waiting does need practice; so all of this aggression will be directed towards a valiant protector and hapless procreator—YOU.

Spot the Kangaroo Dad

As the darkness of daddy-hood creeps up on your life and you are subjected to bouts of stern badgering, another, wiser male of your species is chuckling imperceptibly. Lurking in the recesses of your WhatsApp group, your role model prowls incognito. He indulges, unfettered, in all the recreation that seems to be slipping out of your grasp. Still, he doesn't lose the admiration of onlookers nor the affection of his brood. He moonwalks the Fatherhood Hall of Fame, playfully distracting his progeny and cleverly preserving the adoration of his spouse. He effortlessly attracts the admiration of fellow fathers. This is not the time to doubt the bona fides of this clever, clever specimen. Nor is it the time to grudge this devious character his tradecraft. Rather, it is the time to peek into his playbook, emulate his tactics and mould your strategy based on his mastery. But first, we have to find him.

Recognize that this dexterous comrade might be a bit of a challenge at the start. He operates, after all, in a shroud of social secrecy, practising his dark art in the shadows beyond the glare of social media posts. It is not a skill he can afford to brag or boast about. This is not the kind of thing that will win him any brownie points if spoken about in public. Its discovery can destroy the very fabric of a fulfilling life led outside the purview of spousal supervision. You are more likely to discover the truth about a friend who belongs to the secret society of the Illuminati, or is part of the universal brotherhood of the Freemasons, than unmask this invisible vigilante hiding in plain sight. Part of the reason he's so hard to pick out in a crowd at a children's party or a housing society soiree is that he looks just like you. The same dad-bod that still believes it looks like an aesthetic ideal, the same branded casual apparel bought during sale time, the same credit card rewards programme you are feeling so smug about enrolling in. Yet, peer closely and you will see the one thing that distinguishes him to the keen observer. It's an almost imperceptible feature evident only to the keenest observer of human expression. Did you see it? Look closer. There it is. The corners of his mouth are turned up ever so slightly every now and then. Yes! You can see it now . . . It is his SMILE!

I can understand your confusion at this point. You smile too, you catch yourself thinking. But in comparison with him, your 'smile' is just a tired baring of a few world-weary enamel chunks. His knowing smile, on the other hand, is the self-satisfied, smug smirk of a man in control of his destiny, unshaken by the idiosyncrasies of underage human beings. Combine this with the tendency to wear that dastardly enemy of sartorial grace, the cargo pant, and you know that you have finally spotted him with the visual acuity of an animal tracker in a dense jungle.

Congratulations. You have just spotted a member of the cult of the kangaroo dad. Now all you have to do is emulate him. But first, what is a kangaroo dad and why are we holding him up as the highest form of aspiration for slacker dads? We will now take a slight detour from our study of human behaviour and head into a brief examination of the behavioural patterns of kangaroos.

Kangaroos live in a matriarchal society: the mothers do all the hard work, and the dads are just the breeding bucks. Bucks are not stay-at-home dads or any kind of dads. They return to their families sometimes after six months and it isn't like they are employed during that period. They spend it literally just hopping around. And here is where they ace it: they are greeted with great joy by their young joeys even after a long period of total non-involvement and will win any daddy competition. The mums too are non-judgemental about this cavalier approach to fatherhood. You see now why being a kangaroo dad is ideal? Your kids love you and you didn't even earn it. The mother of your kids is also pretty relaxed about your dalliances with her friends. Pinch yourself; this is all true.

Now we need to get you to be a human version of a kangaroo dad. It is going to be slightly tougher, though, for the following reasons:

1. Monogamy is non-negotiable (these are the rules)
2. You cannot take off for six months; you have to stay put
3. You are not married to a kangaroo (minor detail)

But the end result we want to achieve is the same: you reap all the benefits of being a dad with minimal involvement. Like everything in this book, this comes with a healthy dose of posturing and pretence. But we got this, buddy. By the time we are done, you will be a practised member of the cult of the kangaroo dad.

Here, for the first time ever, we give you the unmasking of the kangaroo dad. Read. Every. Word. This is where you stand at a precarious crossroads. Take the blue pill of denial and your miserable, sleep-deprived, diaper-drenched life remains the same. Swallow the red pill of kangaroo daddy-dom and you will see just how far the rabbit hole to whiskey-infused freedom with your poker pals goes.

Unmasking the Kangaroo Dad

Kangaroo dads are a curious breed. Not only because they operate in permanent stealth mode but also because they manage to create the illusion of effectiveness. Evolutionary psychologists Alan Miller and Satoshi Kanazawa posit that there are more 'deadbeat dads', fathers who shirk their paternal duties, than 'deadbeat moms' because prehistorically, fathers could never be quite sure of whether the offspring was really theirs. This, however, was at a time when Homo sapiens mated freely and intermingled at convenience. Since we are now all bound by duplicitous decency and a societal code of outward monogamy, this does not explain the mythical abilities of the kangaroo dad. Instead, the kangaroo dad is almost boastful of his fatherly prowess. Acutely aware that his reputation would be beaten to death and his cover blown if anyone ever saw him demonstrate deadbeat dad behaviour, the kangaroo dad is the master of the Grand Gesture. Carrying baby, changing nappies, rushing out to buy formula, organizing games at the kiddie party, staying awake at night during a bout of colic pain—these are the staple Grand Gestures of the kangaroo dad. How then is that different from the regular, sleep-deprived, socially isolated dad? And how, if he is engaged in doing all this, can he possibly find the time to stop the decimation of his recreation due to procreation? Because he has impeccable timing. This timing doesn't just refer to the exact moment of the enactment of said Grand Gesture, but also the duration of it.

The Grand Gesture, such as it is, is only ever executed under the glare of public scrutiny: those moments when relatives and friends visit. Those moments when other mummies and daddies are fretting in the playground. That moment when certain bedlam and chaos would ensue at a dinner party if a kangaroo dad didn't take steer of the situation. It is in these fleeting moments that the kangaroo dad comes alive. Not only does he prove his mettle when it is most needed, but these valiant acts of momentary masterfulness exempt him from a life of constant nanny-hood.

Like his marsupial counterpart, a kangaroo dad mates, produces offspring and then scampers about the countryside fulfilling his other pursuits. Like the real kangaroo father, he returns intermittently to the adoring, instinctive affection of his progeny. Encouraged by the various indulgences he showers them with, his brood will skip around the limits of patience, and then, as if to ensure they don't lose his fascination for them, dive headlong into some act of minor rebellion to remind him of the tedium of child-rearing. In an act of firm fatherliness, he will then issue a minor rebuke and admonishment. Partly aimed at the defaulter but mostly at mother dearest, as if to say 'you need to do a better job of child-raising to ensure better manners', the kangaroo dad effectively and swiftly presses the 'maternal guilt' button with particular artfulness. This marks the beginning of a phase of corrective redress by a mother racked with a sense of inadequacy. Once again, the kangaroo dad is free to roam the countryside.

Of course, the tricky part of entering the hallowed kangaroo dad club is becoming a part of a club that is unmentionable. How does one enter a club that no one acknowledges the existence of?

Membership is granted only to the artful few who know the one key tenet of kangaroo dad-ism. Are you ready for it? It is this: kangaroo dad is as kangaroo dad does. That's it. To gain entry is to be a practitioner who acquires expertise by launching headlong into the rewarding practice of being a kangaroo dad and following the eight rules of kangaroo dad-ism. Don't go googling this; it is an arcane code that exists outside the grasp of even the dark web. But since this is the first, only and most definitive guide to the kangaroo dad phenomenon, here, and only here, are the eight rules to being a member of the hallowed kangaroo dad club (to be followed when your child is between zero and three years old).

1. You do not talk about the kangaroo dad club
2. You definitely do not talk about the kangaroo dad club
3. If someone you are married to yells 'stop!' goes limp, or taps out, the kangaroo dad act is over
4. Only two parents to a bottle feed in public
5. One nipple/pacifier at a time
6. All baby-related activities are bare knuckle. No maids, no moms, no gadgets

7. Public displays of affection will go on as long as they have to
8. If this is your first time as a kangaroo dad, you have to change nappies

Now the above holds good for infants and babies (do remember to put up Instagram posts/videos of you doing things for the baby). But the kangaroo dad is too evolved an idea to be abandoned in its infancy. Pun intended. We need to keep honing it. But first, do you have it in you to stay the course? Are you man enough?

Let's recap: you know the phenomenon, you have empirical evidence of its existence, you know the typical traits of a kangaroo dad and now, crucially, you know the rules of kangaroo dad-ism. That leaves only one key gap in your growing body of knowledge. How do you know you have it in you to be a kangaroo dad? How do you know you can attain this level of mastery of the modus operandi of the greatest specimen of fatherhood ever to have charted the course of modern parenting? For your consideration, here are a few scientifically curated archetypical kangaroo dads to help you piece together what kind of a kangaroo dad you can be. Thank me later. Now, dive in and choose your persona.

This is valid for your child in the age group of three to twelve years. As we have discussed previously, after twelve, let us leave the beasts to their own devices.

Kangaroo Dad 1: The All-Terrain Dad

The all-terrain dad (ATD) is the quintessential picnic planner. Over-compensating for days of absence attributable to the feverish pursuit of professional success, the ATD's chief weapon is his trusty SUV. Combined with a second home, ATD is unassailable in his ability to make his paternal neglect a non-issue. Come the weekend, ATD is back, cargo pants and all, loaded with a picnic basket and a cooler of beer cans, to whisk away the attention-deprived brood to the farmhouse. The next few weeks will see more days of ominous absence, but for now, ATD is everywhere. There he is lighting a barbecue fire. There he is setting up the games. There he is putting the dessert and colas out in unending quantities. ATD is so much fun—compared to the mum who can't seem to rise above getting the homework done. He, on the other hand, makes parenting a picnic—literally.

Kangaroo Dad 2: The Jocular Jock

The jocular jock (JJ) has achieved the ability to transfer all his sporting ambitions to his next of kin. Himself a sports enthusiast, he realizes that blending his first love, sports, with his second love, being a kangaroo dad, equals parenting nirvana and makes for enjoyable Facebook posts. By constantly coaching his young ones to attain sporting excellence, he is able to disguise burning ambition as dutiful parenting and keep things interesting for himself. Hold the bat this way. Kick the ball that way. Swing the racket this way. These urgings bring about a keen sense of self-endowed expertise being imparted to the next generation. Onlookers will curl their lips in wonderment, 'Look how he is encouraging sporting excellence at such a young age!' 'This is exactly what will help realize future greatness; what a great dad!' In his mind's eye, JJ can see his own grand future as a world-class sports figure. Another stab at greatness. Thank god for Decathlon's summer sale. The mother, on the other hand, will never have the ambition or imagination to drive her children to attaining these pinnacles; she is much too occupied with the mundane—such as actually bringing them up.

Kangaroo Dad 3: The Brainiac Buddy

The brainiac buddy (BB) is the intellectual twin of the jocular jock. Similar in every respect, his gentle soul masks a competitive spirit. Far from the glare of the stadium's halogen lights, his arena is the battlefield of the mind. Within the four corners of the board game is where his ambition lies. His allies are mind-moulders: chess coaches, Kumon, abacus and Vedic maths trainers. Come little one. Let's open your mind to a world of intellectual snobbery that could make for interesting anecdotes at PTA meetings. The BB has cleverly combined hobby horses with plans for world domination in an age when being a geek is a surety to running the world someday. Something he ruminates about while driving to local chess competitions, general-knowledge quizzes and maths contests. We have no evidence that BB actually helps in unlocking the greatness of his child's mind (there is only so much his genes can do after all), but at least he is doing something more meaningful than working out what goes into their lunch boxes and where the hell you can get a costume from Jharkhand for your four-year-old on her school day. That is the kind of unthinking administrative aspect of parenting that mums should handle.

There you have it: the unlocking of a glorious future and a step towards parenting greatness. Your chance to join a secret fellowship of feckless fathers that allegedly counts towering figures such as Steve Jobs, Brad Pitt and Maradona amongst its number. Be any one of these kangaroo dads. Be any combination of these kangaroo dads. Be all of these kangaroo dads. There's never been a better time to hop on the kangaroo dad bus.

8

How to Be a Likeable Bigot

Before we get into what is likely to be the most critical chapter of this book, it is crucial that we define the following terms: 'bigot' and 'likeable'. These are definitions taken from the Oxford Dictionary; in case of any dispute, feel free to sue it.

> Bigot: A person who has strong, unreasonable ideas, especially about race or religion and who thinks anyone who does not have the same beliefs is wrong.

> Likeable: Readily or easily liked; pleasing.

If you place the meanings side by side, you will realize the challenges of being a likeable bigot in theory. A bigot is a person who puts off people with the strength of their thoughts, which are based not on fact, but on bias. If you put off people, you are not likeable. Simple. So how then do you become a likeable bigot? At this point of time, start with our assurance that a likeable bigot may not be a theoretical possibility—but it is definitely a practical way of life.

In an ideal world, this book would tell you how to be only likeable. Likeability is the key to survival. Sometimes, all you need to make it through life is to be moderately affable. Big corporations often let go of hugely accomplished people because they fail to be affable. A likeable bigot, though, some misguided people would say, apart from being an oxymoron is also a moron. But we are not those hopelessly naïve people. We don't want the world to change. Changing the world is just too much of a chore; at the very most, it will kill you. At the very least, it will give you ulcers. People who want to change the world have the most erratic meal timings: they often skip lunch, driven by a larger cause. But the larger cause has no nutritional value and rebellion only gives you acidity. Bigotry, on the other hand, can be a lot more wholesome given its uncomplicated and one-note nature.

Changing bigotry is well outside the purview of this book. We are not into changing mindsets, ideologies or inborn biases. Neither do we choose to judge you based on them. Keep your bigotry; hold on to your biases. Just make sure you are likeable. Bigotry only has a branding problem and that is what we need to fix. We need to rebrand bigotry and remove the value judgement from it. We need to pedal a softer version of it. Refer back to the meaning of bigotry; the case we build today is that while the ideas behind it may be strong, they are not unreasonable at all—and therefore attaching likeability to it is a reasonable ask.

At this point, we must stress that there is a difference between the likeable bigot and the murderous religious fanatic. Our bigot is not a doer and will never actually *do* anything apart from the odd incoherent tweet. The case we are building then is only for this wholesome, amiable bigot. So if you are an active practitioner of hate crimes or have indulged in moderate to intense levels of genocide, this is not for you. We really don't want Type A personalities here.

Now let's get back on track with the agenda for this chapter.

Here is a step-by-step guide on how to hold on to all your biases, be closed to facts and yet be likeable. In the next few pages we will employ a technique of narrative persuasion where we cast the bigot as the misunderstood good guy. The guy who actually has good intentions, a heart of gold, but is just maligned. The aim is to reposition the bigot as the model of affability, good sense and logic that he or she actually is. Movies do this all the time—get you to invest in a narrative, so after a point, you lose track of reality. We give bigotry its emotional backstory and make you—the bigot—the likeable main lead of your movie.

Here then are the guidelines for a glossy, palatable and crowd-pleasing version of bigotry. These are the various roles that a bigot can play, disproving that he or she is one-note and unidimensional, and is in fact a versatile, multitasking person.

(Please note instructions on facial expressions after every tip. Being chronically pleasant is a strict mandate.)

1. The Bigot as BFF (Best Friends Forever, Not Bigot Forever)

As a card-holding bigot, when you are putting forth a slightly problematic view on a race, religion, gender or sexuality, always preamble it with, 'Some of my best friends are . . . ' This also means you have to be slightly indiscriminate in the use of the phrase 'best friends', but that could be the least of your character flaws. So don't dwell on it.

Example
a) What you say: Some of my best friends are Muslims and they are really nice people person-to-person, but you know that religion is only a bit hardcore.
(What you really mean: You know a couple of nice Muslim blokes, but they can't all help being fanatical nutters. The 'niceness' of the people you know might be a function of your niceness, just by the way.)
The other alternative to this is 'Not everybody is, but the fact is . . . ' There is actually no fact in your assertion, but don't let that stop you from liberally using this phrase.

Example

b) What you say: Not all women are emotional in the workplace, but the fact is that they just can't compartmentalize the personal and the professional. (*What you really mean: Women are emotional wrecks to deal with in the workplace.*)

(Smile.)

2. The Intellectual Bigot aka the Gobbledygookist

If you are equipped to, always use words that come couched in intellectualism. Words such as 'equivalence' and 'sociopolitical narrative' and 'apperceptive background'. If you sound incredibly erudite, nobody will catch on to hidden biases. Don't be too bombastic, though, because we still need you to be likeable—and no pompous stuffed shirt is liked much.

Complicate the narrative. The more oblique you are, the easier it will be for you to hold on to and reinforce biases.

Example

a) Some of my best friends are Muslims and I can vouch for them, but you need to examine the socio-religious construct they are a part of to understand the primacy of faith in their lives. (*Subtext: All Muslims, best friends included, are fanatical nutters or have the potential to be.*)

b) Not all women are emotional in the workplace, but you need to view them through the prism of their apperceptive backgrounds and understand that capitulation to emotion is part of the female psyche.
(Subtext: All women are emotional wrecks in the workplace.)

Basically, the aim here is to always speak in finely constructed gobbledygook. You are likeable, you are bigoted and you also sound intelligent. You make it sound as if your bigotry has an academic basis to it, that you have arrived at it after careful analysis and theoretical rigour. It isn't personal; it is in fact a detached, philosophical internalization of bigotry.

(Keep smiling.)

3. The Logical Bigot

When someone like you—read someone from your community—commits a crime or misdemeanour, it is clearly an individual aberration. If someone outside your community does the same, he or she indicts the entire race or religion he or she belongs to. Always be equipped with infallible logic like this that can't be countered. The advantage of having an opinion not based on facts is that it can't be countered by facts. Don't overreach by attempting to actually research your closely held beliefs.

That is a foolish move and might shake our convictions. We don't want to do that. We want status quo.

(Hold that smile.)

4. The Inclusive and Questioning Bigot

Always ask the right questions, which, in your case, begin and end with 'but what about?'

The social media phenomenon of 'whataboutery' comes under a lot of fire from hostile liberals. 'What about' is a question that is often misunderstood as a deflection tactic; it is in fact inclusive and shows a generosity of spirit. When a misdeed or crime in committed in the name of your community or religion, always make sure to be inclusive and do a headcount of all other crimes committed in the name of other religions or communities. Our point is to be all-embracing and say that criminals come from different religions. It is just that when it is one of ours, he is a misguided individual, but when it is one of yours, all you guys are the same. That is just the way it is. Deal with it. Our gods have different interests and yours seem to like crime and terror slightly more.

Therefore, as a perfectly reasonable bigot, when it comes to dealing with crimes committed by two different communities, make sure to point out that even if the crime is similar, the perpetrator is not. A white murderous man is a dysfunctional teddy bear. A black murderous man or a brown one with a skullcap was just born that way. Four men sent profane photos to a female journalist. One of them was from a different community. All the men were creeps, but that particular man was guided by his religion to be a creep.

Create a Selective Equivalence

Here is the tricky part. You have to be artful in the creation of an equivalence. In the above example, you are dodging it. But there are times when you need to use it. Be discriminate in your use of it. Not all situations are equal, but with crafty selection you can bring about parity.

Example 1: A murder is committed. The motivations are religious. A killed B because B was of a different religion. The religion of the perpetrator is therefore a factor that will be reported on.

Example 2: Now C, who is of the same religion as B, kills A. However, C kills A because A defaulted on a loan. The religion of the perpetrator is not a factor or motive and therefore logically should not be reported on or highlighted.

Now, this is precisely the kind of logic we cannot encourage. Examples 1 and 2 are exactly the same and if you can attack my religion based on the first case, the second needs the same approach and also becomes about religion. Otherwise, it is clearly a case of bleeding-heart selective liberalism and pseudo liberalism. A true liberal will acknowledge the equivalence. This is a masterly move because you have successfully addled logic with a persuasive emotional pitch. You ask the compelling question: either the religion of the perpetrator counts in all cases or it doesn't count in any. How can this position be argued with? It makes for such solid good sense. How can holding this position be an example of bigotry and not liberalism in its truest sense, instead of the elitist, Western concepts that we seem to love so much? It is also always a good idea to introduce this element of Western imposition into the mix.

Facts Are Friends

Don't get too rattled by facts. Facts, in fact, can be your biggest ally in holding on to bigotry. A bit of a crash course in psychology now and something called 'The Backfire Effect'. What it essentially means is that when a pet set of beliefs or opinions is contradicted by facts, your opinion will not change. It will in fact become stronger. Here is the thing: we are inherently lazy. We spend a considerable amount of time building a certain belief or value system. To dismantle it is too much effort. So instead of examining the validity of a counter opinion, we look for 'facts' that will confirm our biases. And hold on to our biases. This book recognizes that and therefore will make no attempt to change your biases. All we aim to do is to help ensure that as a practising bigot, you are at least generally amiable.

(Smile wider. More teeth. Perfect.)

5.   The Bigot as Free-Speech Advocate

Strictly speaking, a bigoted view is a view that has the right to be expressed. Our Constitution guarantees freedom of expression. Hold on to this right and use it strategically. A lot of deep thinkers will tell you that if you don't call out bigotry amongst friends, family and colleagues, you are part of the problem. You are normalizing it. It is at this point that you can confuse the issue and in fact take the higher moral ground. Tell them you will not shout down alleged bigotry as every value system has a right to exist in a robust democracy. You support freedom of expression. Keep this quote handy, which you must misattribute to Voltaire: 'I disapprove of what you say, but I will defend to death your right to say it.' Apparently, Voltaire didn't say this; someone else did. But we don't want to be too strong on facts, so never mind that.

(Perilously close to smiling your head off now.)

6.   The Bigot as Marketer

At the very outset, we have set out our express purpose. Bigotry needs a massive rebranding exercise. You need to soft sell it. How do you do this? By giving it softer labels such as 'controversial', 'provocative', 'contentious', 'fractious', 'problematic', 'conservative' or 'old school'. This relabelling makes it part of the mainstream narrative and socially acceptable. It takes the edge off the issue and puts forward the proposition that a bigot is just another kind of person expressing a different opinion. It could be the jovial uncle on the family WhatsApp group or it could be the college friend on Facebook or it could be you. You are not a bigot; you are just another type of person with a slightly different take. And hey, isn't the new world order about diversity and inclusiveness? You see what you have done there: not only have you normalized being a bigot, you have also made it a part of a larger scheme of diversity.

(Smile your head off.)

7. A Bigot Is a Liberal Turned Inside Out—Just a Lot Nicer. #SameGuy

A bigot and a hard-nosed liberal will have contrasting and divergent views. Focus on the commonality. Both of these views are hardliner views. What you need to do is hone in on the hardliner part: you need to state that you are opposed to extreme opinion and would rather seek the middle ground. The middle ground is a grey area, a moral marshmallow that will be more acceptable to the bigot and untenable to the liberal. You can then make a case for how inflexible the liberal is and is therefore more of the deviant than the bigot. The context for the hardliner views does not matter. The fact that they are often non-negotiable is what you can deflect the attention to.

Example: (This is an amended version of a popular Internet meme clearly made by a liberal.)

Bigot: All people from XYZ community have criminality in their blood.

Liberal: That is an irrational thing to say. No person from that community is a born criminal.

You: These are both extreme positions. Can we please find a middle ground?

Liberal: There is no middle ground on something like this.

Bigot: Okay. Most of them are born criminals.

You: Should we say some?

Liberal: No.

Bigot: Okay. Some of them are born criminals.

You: Great. We have reached a consensus.

Liberal: No. We haven't. I don't agree.

You: Well, he is not the problem then. You are. Your stance is inflexible.

Do an unemotional think: who would you rather have running the world, the inflexible liberal who leaves no room for negotiation or the amenable to reason bigot who is willing to relax his stance? I would say vote for the reasonable, likeable guy—the bigot.

(Smile heading into laugh zone.)

8. The Flexible Bigot

This is a masterstroke in the art of psychological warfare. Your biggest ally in this is not a fellow bigot or an ambivalent bigot. It can be the super-woke, super-strident liberal. This is a person who believes in absolutes and hard sells an apocalyptic vision of the world. This person also operates in an echo chamber where anyone who doesn't share his or her views is a bigot. This inflexibility makes it easier for an amiable version of bigotry to flourish. It will dismiss a popular mandate as collective insanity; it will mourn and whine but not have any coherent strategy besides composing smart tweets, which never won anyone anything.

What they do then is effectively work in a closed circle—one where people leaning towards a more complex and nuanced stance are not welcome. As a result, the silent, shunned moderate gets clubbed with the bigot. And finally, it is a volumes game. Right now, the bigots have the numbers. What they can rest assured in is that there will be no resistance: the liberal is in a prolonged sulk. All we therefore need to focus on is making your bigotry likeable. By the time we are done, you will be winning all of those congeniality contests.

The liberal, in the meanwhile, will be thinking of a suitable dire meme to post from *Game of Thrones* on

Twitter. You don't need to worry about them. They are sulky space cadets without a plan (the chapter on 'How to Be a Sulking Liberal' follows).

(Laugh out loud now.)

9. Bigots as Fake-News-Busters

Bigots don't have a jaundiced view of journalism based on facts; journalism itself is yellow. Bigots are blessed with an inborn filter, which helps them differentiate between fake news and news that really matters. They use this indiscriminately—and they should because the world needs to be saved from the tyranny of agenda-driven facts.

Go by your hidden instincts, biases and gut. These are always more powerful than plain old facts. The factual narrative of the media cannot be a substitute for the uncanny instinct you have for the actual state of things. The media that constantly plays up an odd case of bigotry or two is the problem, and not the bigotry itself. Fortunately for us, we live in times when a significant portion of the media too believes in gut over fact. And therefore, will actually not report on facts. The section that does is clearly biased and looking for easy clicks. We can choose to ignore their reportage. The reportage of the incidents is the problem; the fact that they occur is not. There will always be the odd one, or odd one hundred, or odd one million cases of bigotry. Do we really need to highlight and amplify them? Get your priorities right. Focus on the positives. Refer to chapter on 'How to Be a Chronic Feel-Gooder'.

(Go back to smiling widely.)

10. The Desh-Bhakt Bigot

At this stage, we will again pull out the Oxford Dictionary and define what a nationalist is.

> Nationalist: A person who strongly identifies with their own nation and vigorously supports its interests, especially to the exclusion or detriment of the interests of other nations.

Please go back to the beginning of the chapter and read the definition of 'bigot' again. You see that line—it is blurred a bit, isn't it? Blur it further so that the bigot metamorphoses into a nationalist. You are a nationalist, and you believe in the sanctity of your country and culture. You are the sort of person people make movies on and write books about. You are completely right in calling out people who don't share your patriotic fervour. It doesn't make you a bigot. And it also makes you very likeable—to the extent that you could soon run for public office.

(Add a semi-smirk to the smile.)

11. The Bigot Has the Last Laugh

Satire and humour can be another key accomplice in spreading our beatific version of bigotry. A bigot is too straitlaced a person to use satire. It is far too twisted and complicated a device. But contrary to what you think, we can actually use it to further the interests of bigotry.

As far back as 2011, a study by scholars at Ohio State University examined how satire such as *The Colbert Report* 'registered differently among liberals and conservatives— how humour is filtered through certain predispositions'. The conclusion was that satire often reinforced one's existing beliefs; in very lay terms, one saw only what one wanted to see. So all those woke comedians doing their fine satirical pieces running down bigotry only strengthen our existing biases. Bigots are far too sweet and simple to be able to tell satire and take humour at face value. The more you run it down in a humorous, oblique fashion, the more convinced they are about their worldview.

You see then why this chapter is a masterstroke.

(As the legit likeable bigot, proceed to the last laugh now.)

Therefore, in conclusion, there is nothing to stop a bigot from scaling the popularity charts because as we have conclusively proved, he or she is not hidebound or ignorant but guided by reason, inclusiveness and a sense of fair play and is deeply patriotic.

What's not to like?

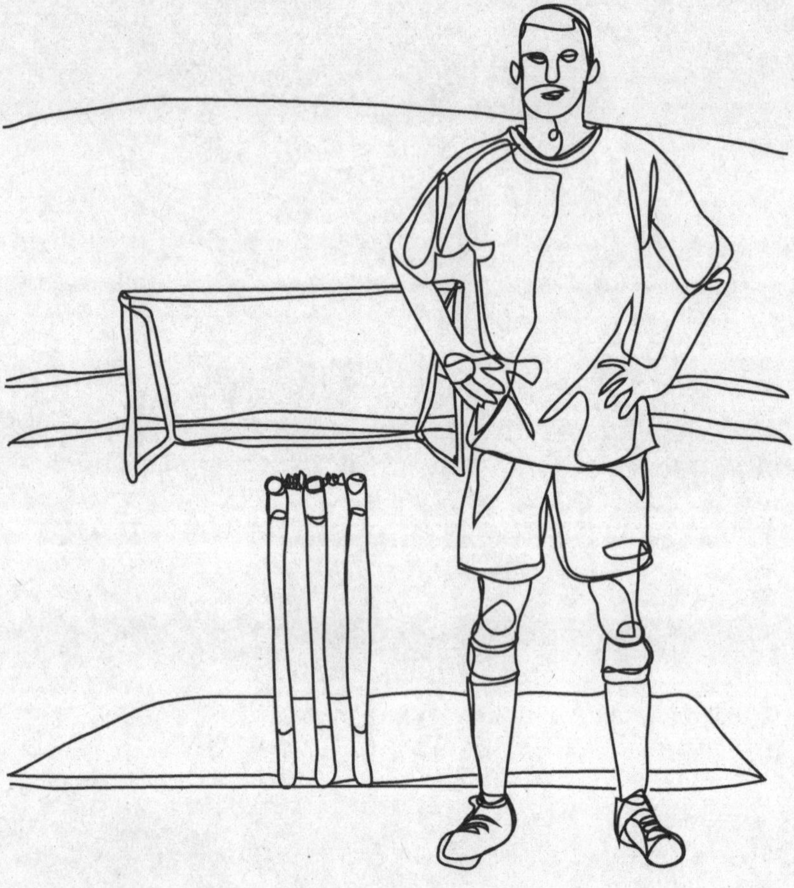

9

How to Be a Sulking Liberal

At my undergraduate level, I found myself taking philosophy as an elective. As this book must have amply demonstrated by now, I am not a person who is given to deep thinking or philosophical inquiry. However, I took up the subject because I was told it would be easy to score in and give me enough time to focus on my major, English literature. I don't remember much of what we studied (though I did score well, which was always the plan), but I do remember a standing joke the class had on the French philosopher Descartes. He had famously written, '*Cogito, ergo sum,*' which means, 'I think, therefore, I am.' What Descartes meant was that by the very act of doubting one's existence, one is proving one's existence. The fact that you have the ability to think means you exist. As teenagers, we had many variations of it: 'I eat, therefore, I am', 'I have a pimple, therefore, I am', 'I belch, therefore, I surely am'. We discovered many trivial rationales for our trivial existence and found each a lot more hilarious than they actually were. Descartes wouldn't have been amused. And since he is already unamused, I may as well take the liberty of extending the flippancy of our teenage years to the state of the modern-day liberal—an intrepid, fearless and slightly whiny social media warrior.

The Indian liberal can be summed up thus, 'I sulk, therefore, I am'—and that is his or her only plan: petulance. It is pretty comfortable being a liberal: you live in an air-conditioned echo chamber and then Uber it to other echo chambers. You sip tea out of eco-friendly earthen pots with other suitably stirred individuals and lament the end of reason. You shudder and wring your hands in delicate distaste at the ignorant masses and hope the right hashtag will bring back the world order you so desire. You haven't really defined what that world order is; it is a bit hazy, but you know it is sweet and flaky—a bit like you. It is a charming place where people waft around in wishy-washy congeniality, saying perfectly well-mannered things to each other.

Mostly, this book is not about specific events or people, but in setting forth the manifesto of the sulking liberal in India, I will have to reference topical events and set out a structured plan of action. A structured plan of action is exactly the kind of thing our lofty liberal has no idea about. It is much too workmanlike for him. Actually, the sulking liberal is even less of a doer than our amiable bigot. The bigot has the force of his convictions. The liberal is mostly confused about what his convictions are—but he knows that whatever they are, they make him morally superior to the rest of humanity. The liberal, then, is clearly not a person of action and is in fact the ideal reader of this book.

But first, let us identify the 'sulking liberal'. This is a particular breed you will find almost exclusively on social media. Usually eloquent in English, they use many pop-culture references, are cosmopolitan and a citizen of the world. They are very self-aware of their position—usually a privileged one. But are deluded enough to imagine that by constantly reminding themselves of it on Twitter and Facebook, they have somehow reduced the burden of their privilege. And are now kindred spirits with the marginalized, the dispossessed and the actual social activists.

Now for some context, and as they say, a backstory for the state of the Indian liberal.

In April 2019, India went to the polls. The BJP-led NDA headed by Prime Minister Narendra Modi was bidding for a second innings after a sweeping mandate in 2014. The intervening five years had its highs and lows, but what was being chronicled by worried liberals was a growing wave of Hindu nationalism and hate crimes against minorities. The entire country, they had concluded, was turning rabid and needed to be saved from itself. That was the only thing that was happening in the country; nothing else mattered. This is an incredibly surface explanation of the liberal mindset, but it is only to set context, so we will keep to it. To be fair, the liberal was not being unduly paranoid: there is/was an atmosphere that seemed to be pushing liberal values into a corner. Back to our story then:

113

it wasn't expected to be easy for the ruling party at the polls—at least Indian Twitter didn't think so. The BJP won 303 Lok Sabha seats—a rousing mandate and a thumping majority. Turns out the liberals didn't have a clue about what happens beyond their Facebook walls.

The liberal reaction was one of dismay, which soon turned into disdain for anything that even slightly countered their narrative of impending anarchy. The disdain soon converted into a hostile suspicion of anyone who didn't subscribe to the doomsday predictions. It meant shunning anyone or anything that didn't fit in with their world view. This refusal to engage with multiple narratives and opinions made sense: you were outnumbered. You might as well make yourself irrelevant as well. This is often called the paradox of liberalism or illiberal liberalism, where a liberal shouts down a contrarian view because he or she operates on the assumption that their stance is the only one worth having. Everyone else is a yokel. A truly democratic stance.

That brings us to our first defining characteristic written in the first person for no particular reason.

1. There Is Only One Reality—Mine!

I only accept multiple realities in films bankrolled by Hollywood studios. In real life, there is only one reality. Mine. And in that reality, I am constantly on a moral high ground and will generalize furiously from it. I am overly concerned with monitoring what you think, and like my frenemy, the bigot, am quick to jump to conclusions. Either you are on my side or you are racist, bigoted, a misogynist, a bhakt and worse still—you probably hate cats. I choose not to be pragmatic because that is a cop-out and the middle ground is below my intellectual level. I will not stop demonizing you because if I stop, I lose my reason for existence—my moral superiority. I will not listen to your rationale without flying into a noble, uplifting rage. I don't even realize that by closing myself to differing views, I am pushing myself into a corner. But it is my corner and I light it up with my halo.

In a piece written in 2017 for the *Economist*, author and libertarian Claire Fox said this about the American liberal in a post-Trump world:

> In fact, liberals will only become liberal again once they abandon this type of sneering and smearing and recognize that free speech—even for those we despise—is the core liberal project. Without it, the much feared (often exaggerated) rise of the far-right won't be the biggest threat to our freedoms. Instead, illiberalism, in the name of liberalism, will be the PC midwife of authoritarianism.

2. I Am Generally Clueless but I Am Still Superior to You

Now for the other differentiating features. Please pay close attention. Because, for the most part, the liberal and the bigot look exactly the same. Another stand-out feature of the sulking liberal: an endearing, smug cluelessness. It really is quite cute. You are clueless, but you are clueless that you are clueless and therefore smug.

As the liberal slumped into shock after the verdict of 2019, he did what he does best. In fact, he does this better than the bigot. He made a generalization that was the grandmother of all generalizations. The entire electorate was demonized as bigots. The grief was intense and self-involved. How had your tweets not stopped this country from its rapid descent into fascism? It was confounding. To be a sulking liberal, therefore, it is key that at all times you don't get over yourself and your inflated sense of self-worth.

It is quite simple—people who didn't buy into my non-plan are to blame. I don't have a plan. I am rudderless. But I am the good guy, so you must buy into my plan. If you don't, you are a bigot. There is no way anything else could have motivated your vote but your hatred for minorities. It couldn't be development, strong governance, stability or just the lack of options. I am not buying that. I gave you an option. I said anyone but that guy who seems to have a plan. Okay, it wasn't an option, I agree. But that is your problem. You are the bad guy and guess what, we are no longer Facebook friends. Yes—go figure.

3. I Am a Whiner with No Grace

The third differentiating feature of a sulking liberal: an utter lack of grace. Always be utterly graceless in dissing the majority as ignorant, fascist and unenlightened. Spread bleakness. A popular election and free will have given you a government, but do go ahead with your memes on an apocalypse coming your way. Harry Potter and *Avengers: Infinity War* quotes on fighting the forces of evil are just what you need to stop fascism in its tracks. Well played.

4. I Am Too Cool to Be a Patriot

I am a bit uncomfortable about patriotism. It seems plebeian. I detect in it signs of jingoism, which gives me the shivers. I, therefore, don't watch sports and especially not cricket. I constantly scold euphoric sporting victory tweets for their exuberance. It is a tad vulgar to exult in sporting triumph as it is interlinked to a showy brand of hyper-nationalism.

You: Yay. We totally trashed Pakistan today. Go home, losers.

Me: I refuse to see sports as a substitute for war. I cannot be a hyena baying for the blood of the enemy on a sporting field. I would rather you spoke on the quality of goals that the Indian side scored. I would rather the triumph be internalized and lead to introspection on the fleeting nature of victory.

You: I can't possibly do that.

Me (interrupting in tones of deep contempt): Of course you can't; it is not the sport that interests you. It is a shallow sense of the superiority of your nation, which can finally only be self-defeating . . .

You: I can't talk about the goals the Indian side scored because it was a cricket match.

Me (past caring and past hearing): Who are you? Who is this person you have become? Do I even know you any more?

You (quietly skulks off to have coffee with the likeable bigot instead. The bigot, in a fit of misattributed national pride, is paying. For the coffee and the cookie.)

I, in the meanwhile, have written a verbose convoluted Twitter thread on sports as a tool of fascism. I draw parallels from the discourse on Leni Riefenstahl's stirring documentary *Olympia* on the 1936 Berlin Olympics, which is often referred to as a Nazi propaganda film. Unfortunately, not one right-winger trolls me as none of them understand it.

5. I Say Majoritarianism a Lot

I like saying majoritarianism. It took me some time to master the spelling, but I have aced it. Majoritarianism, besides being a mouthful, means that the numerical majority of a population should have the final say in determining an outcome. That is what I have a problem with because I believe the majority cannot be left to govern themselves. This does make me inflexible and is on the face of it, an autocratic view. But then, being a liberal is complicated.

6. I Have Difficulty in Calling Out Everything Equally

In an ideal world, the liberal should be taking slingshots at everything and everyone that are the opposite of liberal values. We choose to be discerning and selective. Kashmiri Pandits being driven out of their homes and the second-class citizenship given to non-tribal residents in parts of the Northeast are not things we want to rage about because the aggressors are prime objects of affection of our bleeding hearts. We will sneer at women fasting for the long lives of their husbands as a regressive imposition, but a young actor turning away from her career because religion came in the way is freedom of choice. The gaze is patriarchal in both cases for both communities—but my liberal heart knows there is a difference. I also know what to say to those who call out my bleeding heart. This is a fake equivalence.

7. I Don't Actually Understand Secular

I don't get that being secular doesn't mean you don't have a religion. You have a religion, but you believe that all religions have the same rights as yours. It doesn't mean I demur from any kind of religious symbolism or rituals. Not believing in organized religion and being an atheist is an individual call, but it is not the mandate of being a liberal. I don't get that, and therefore I am always queasy around religion. I am a bit straitlaced and one-note that way, a bit like the bigot. You didn't hear me say that.

The above pretty much sums up my prolonged sulk as a liberal. I have no plans of doing anything else, because I feel I am doing enough by blocking people on Facebook and then writing moralizing posts on why it broke my heart to find out that my school friend was a bigot. I am not great company to be with, but I can't be complacent and insular like the lot of you. I will often say this is not my country without realizing that I was probably running a country of my own in my head—because this is precisely what my country is. It didn't change overnight. And now, I haven't a clue what to do, because I have pushed away people who could have been on my side with my militant hostility to their point of view.

Leave me then to my devices; I am in an intellectual and moral stupor.

PS: I quite enjoy it. Wake me up when the apocalypse comes.

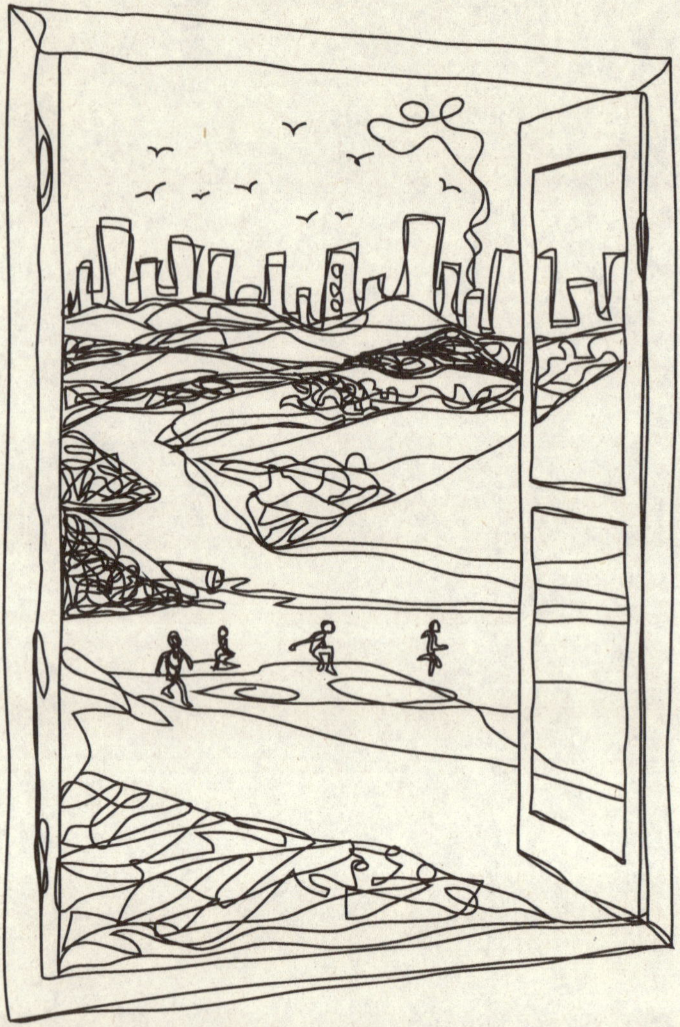

10

How to Be a Chronic Feel-gooder

You haven't read the title of this chapter wrong. A typo hasn't inadvertently crept in; it isn't the printer's devil at work here. This chapter tells you how to be a feel-gooder—not a do-gooder. At the cost of sounding repetitive, we don't want to have much to do with *doing* because that is activity, which will have some sort of consequences. We don't want consequences. We are not pro-activity. We are pro status quo. If it ain't broke, don't fix it. Even if it is broke, don't fix it. After a bit, people will forget it is broke—and life will chug on as usual, as it always unfailingly does.

Remember one key thing as a person who would rather things didn't change: nobody ever wants to change stuff in a vacuum. The triggers for change always come from the environment around you. Something disturbs you, disrupts your routine, doesn't feel right and then you act to change it. Change finally then boils down to that feeling: you *don't* feel good. That is inimical to what this book seeks to achieve. And, therefore, as custodians of a world order that we want to more or less remain the same, we have to focus on making you feel good. Come what may. Because if you *feel* good, you won't *do* a thing.

In principle, there is absolutely nothing wrong with a general feeling of positivity or well-being. If the prevailing circumstances around you are that utopian, you are well within your rights to be perpetually high on life. But sadly, life is never an idyll, which is why we need to work on placing you in a bubble of insular positivity that has no relation with ground reality. The best kind of deception is self-deception and we are here to help you achieve just that.

Focus on the Intangible

As I write this, we are bang in the middle of the monsoons in Mumbai. My house overlooks a river, which is now a gutter. Choked with plastic, it always overflows, inundating the land around it. Mumbai is run by the richest municipal corporation in the country and yet every year the body is routinely surprised by the routine—the monsoons. Roads get jammed, subways get waterlogged and the financial capital of the country announces a public holiday because its government cannot ensure that your daily commute is safe. This happens every year unfailingly, and there is no public protest. There is some outrage on social media, but people on Twitter spend far more time outraging on an inconsequential Bollywood blockbuster. So, that is really that.

Every year, the attention then moves from infrastructure that is teetering and dangerous to something that is unbroken, intangible and feel-good: the Spirit of Mumbai. It is a mythical thing—this spirit that makes a city get back on its feet, no matter what. It apparently differentiates this ruined helpless bustle of a city from other teeming, less-hardy cities. It also does an odd thing: it shifts attention from the failure of the state machinery to individual positivity and achievement. The onus to live in this city and be a beacon of positivity while you are at it is squarely then on you. The state is a spectator; you, on the other hand, are an ambassador of positivity and your collective spirit will buoy you through—and it does every year. The Spirit of Mumbai is an extreme case of feel-good; it is a collective hallucination that goads you to feel good in spite of all evidence to the contrary. The key takeaway in the most dire of situations then becomes optimism and feel-good. It becomes a story about the triumph of the collective human spirit—and not about staggering administrative failure.

The Naysayer vs the Yaysayer

Now if an entire battle-weary and hard-nosed city can happily go along with this illusion of a guardian spirit presiding over it, imagine how much easier it will be for you to build this illusion of cheer and optimism for yourself on an individual level. I now need to introduce a writer whose book partially sparked off an understanding of the phenomenon of the feel-gooder for me: American writer Anand Giridharadas and his book *Winners Take All: The Elite Charade of Changing the World*. What he says in his book is a lot more evolved and erudite, but since this is also the lazy person's guide to social commentary, I will break it down to the very basic. In a chapter titled 'The Critic and the Thought Leader', he quotes extensively from Daniel Drezner, a foreign-policy writer, to make a valuable point. He says the thought economy has been hampered by the replacement of public intellectuals by thought leaders. What is the difference? Public intellectuals are disruptive, anti-establishment and duty-bound to point out chinks in the armour. Thought leaders are pro status quo, brimming with optimism and anecdotal advice; they are not here to point out the chinks. They are, in fact, the armour. It is the naysayer versus the yaysayer, the commentator vs the cheerleader. The Spirit of Mumbai by that extension is a thought leader and will soon have a TED Talk of its own. A forum of hope and positivity that as Giridharadas says, leaves 'little space for criticism or rebuttal, and emphasize hopeful solutions over systemic change'. This is the era of the thought leader. This is the era of the ideas evangelist. This is the era of the feel-gooder. There has never been a better time to feel good—or a worse time.

Staying with what has been said about TED Talks and other such essentially feel-good forums, I have a parallel.

They fill the space in our lives that *Readers' Digest* filled in our parents' lives. I grew up scouring the magazine, basking in the conservatism of its happy, shining middle-class values. It was an advertisement for a sanitized world where, even if adversity showed up, the human spirit always prevailed. It made you feel gently triumphant at all given times. It never told you the system was broken; it said you were unbroken.

And that is the aim of this chapter—our relentless obsession with feeling good and how we can keep it intact. Because in this pursuit, we need to be a bit like *Readers' Digest*: positive, optimistic, cut off from reality and living life in a gentle whirr of mild euphoria.

You do know what will happen next. We have fallen into a nice little pattern, you and I. It is time to present a step-by-step guide to feeling good.

1. Read this book. You already are, but a little bit of hard sell never killed anyone.
2. Do not consume news that is against your belief system. Your belief system has been firmly put in place by WhatsApp forwards, which are the gospel. Do not change that.
3. Always substitute logic with emotion. No one can argue with emotion.
4. Focus relentlessly on the positive. You are not overweight; you are an ambassador for body positivity. You can't hold on to a job because the

rat race is futile. You are non-materialistic. You are never the problem. You are the solution. And as an eminent philosopher of our times said, 'If you can't be the solution, be the precipitate' (Navjyot Singh Sidhu, last seen in a bear hug with Pakistan army chief, General Qamar Javed Bajwa, exuding positivity).

5. Seek constant self-validation through Instagram and Facebook. If you surround yourself with positivity, you will attract more positivity.

6. By the same token, get off Twitter. You could try writing occasional Twitter threads on the humanity of Uber drivers, though. That always works. You could try a bit of irrational outrage. That pumps you up considerably. It does make you feel good. Don't do it too often. It will give you acidity.

7. Be nationalistic. It is a guaranteed feel-good high. Invest all your pride in symbols of national pride like the Indian Army and the Indian cricket team. Especially do this if you are a news journalist or a news editor. Be unquestioning. You will sleep well at night.

8. Your parents needed cinema to escape life—you don't need to do that. You have Netflix. But only patronize or make films that don't disturb the perfect equilibrium we have found in our lives. Stay away from poverty porn; those are films made for whiny festivals.

9. Self-involvement is actively encouraged. Nothing you do in your life is minor or inconsequential. Your life is geared towards making you feel good. The world owes you to feel good. Think of everything in your life as a potential TED Talk. You are your biggest cheerleader.

Think X

I am a mildly optimistic person on a bad day, and a rabid daydreamer otherwise. Once this book becomes the sensation it is destined to be, I envision a series of feel-good workshops and talks based on this chapter. I am calling this series 'Think X'. This will be a platform for people who always miss the cloud for the silver lining. It will make your most mundane, thoughtless gestures a noble, uplifting mission—with an empowering, enlightening message for humanity. It will be my cult of the feel-gooders. I have already begun speaking to people to join up (that way we don't waste too much time when the book acquires cult status). Here are some of the people whose lives I have already impacted and roped in for Think X. Names have been changed to protect identities.

Case study 1: Anita. Twenty-four years old. Mildly overweight. Serial dieter. Compulsive diet cheater. Tries keto intermittently. Indulgent parents pay for every new nutritionist.

(I have signed up young Anita for a Think X talk titled 'My Complex Relationship with Carbs and How I Emerged Stronger'.)

Excerpts from the Think X: *(In Anita's words)*

As I negotiated my relationship with food, I was racked by my complex take on carbohydrates. I was addicted. I couldn't do without them. And the carbs knew they wielded that power over me. Every time, I hopelessly capitulated to just that little bit of pizza or that solitary French fry. But then I changed the power equation—because that is what you do in a toxic, controlling relationship. I told that carb, you don't eat me. I eat you. I said that each time there was a croissant, wafers or a pizza. I looked it in the eye and said slowly, 'You don't eat me. I eat you.' It was my power move. It set me free. I had control, not the carbs. I ate every bit of them, and I felt good. That is the mantra I give to you today. Put yourself in charge; take control. You are not weak. Show your food who is in charge. You are doing the eating. It doesn't get to choose. You do. You will never feel better.

(Anita hasn't lost any weight and is not likely to. However, that is immaterial. She is a testament to food positivity and should be out with her bestselling book soon. I Showed Pizza Who Was Boss. *Her power chant, meanwhile, is an anthem in body-positivity communes the world over.)*

Case study 2: Arjun. Forty years old. Newly divorced. Online dating glutton. Can be mistaken for being slightly 'despo'.

(*Arjun came to me for advice and I state in all humility that I transformed his life.*)

Arjun: So the deal is I have a new Tinder date every night, and I have an 80 per cent strike rate.

Me: That is more than the course of your entire marriage. What are you complaining about?

Arjun: I feel like I am coming across as oversexed and a bit of a 'despo' uncle type.

Me: That might be because you are . . . so not. We have to change this to a life-affirming experience—where this becomes a victory of your spirit and not your libido.

(Arjun looks sceptical and is also preoccupied with swiping right furiously on his phone.)

Me: Do a Think X for me. Talk about your online dating life. It will show you as an evolved, thinking person—deeply sensitive and empathetic. It will be ballsy of you to do it. And please overlook that below-the-belt pun.

Arjun: Sensitive and empathetic. Are you seriously nuts?

Me (in a trance): Thirty dates. Thirty different women. How a newly divorced man discovered truths about himself that a ten-year marriage didn't show him.

Arjun (buying in slowly): What truths did I discover about myself?

Me: That you do need a cycle of empty sex to get over a failed relationship. And yet, it is misleading to call it empty because in the meaninglessness of it, you will penetrate to deeper meaning. You will have life-affirming revelations that you will use to make equally horny men feel good about themselves.

Arjun: Okay. If you put it that way, it does feel really good. I am in.

(Arjun has been signed up for a Think X talk on 'The Healing Power of Empty Sex—My Experiment with Rampant Fornication'. It is bit difficult to tell you in words the impact of his talk, but it does choke up people and is easily one of our more popular talks. Surprisingly, a lot of women attend and Arjun is becoming a bit of a thinking woman's sex symbol. They also willingly participate in further experiments that Arjun has undertaken in the field. All for a good cause. All to reaffirm the larger purpose of human existence.)

Case study 3: Vinod. Traveller. Blogger. Skinflint. Doesn't have the money to stay in a youth hostel, never mind Airbnb.

Here is how Vinod manages free stays in all the cities he visits. And nobody thinks he is a pile-on. Instead, they think he is a humanitarian bringing diverse people together. It usually starts with a social media post.

Here is what he says:

Hi. As the world becomes an increasingly impersonal place, when was the last time you looked up from your phone and spoke to a stranger in the offline world? When was the last time you tried to step out of your comfort zone and stepped into the unfamiliar? There is a risk of judgement and there is a risk of rejection; do you have it in you to risk it? I do. I am conducting a social experiment. I am in your city for two days, and I don't want the homogeneity of a hotel room. Will you let me into your house and your private space? Will we learn from each other? Will we sit—two perfect strangers over a cup of tea—like two old friends and chat about our lives? No agendas. No judgement. I will tell you my travel stories. I will open my heart. Will you too? Will you let a stranger in? I will eat what you eat. I will live the way you do. And in my own way, I will bring down the barriers between 'us' and 'them'.

(DM me. I am travelling in two days. Let's do this.)

Here is what he means:

Hi. I am a skinflint. I want to travel but really don't have the money to. Will you let me bum a stay in your house? I know it sounds creepy, but we could do some Instagram stories on it and I am quite sure BuzzFeed will do a piece on us. I just need a place to crash for two nights—and some time to take some selfies with you, so that credulous people on social media buy into my tale of humanity and positivity. Will you? Will you let a stranger in? Besides my propensity to pile on, I am quite harmless. I will probably need meals too. However, I will get my own toothbrush.

(I am a bit desperate. The first DM I get, I am in.)

Needless to say, Vinod always manages to get a free stay in every city and BuzzFeed does a story on him every month.

(Vinod will also be conducting my Think X talk. He was a bit difficult to get in touch with, but his management team finally confirmed. His session is called 'When Strangers Let You In'. It is also a popular weekly podcast.)

The above case studies should reinforce how putting a positive spin on everything can give a larger, lofty purpose to everything. Don't seek out the ugly, the tacky and the tawdry. Look for hope and feel good. Always feel good.

I walk to my window then and stare at the gutter that was once a river, but there are children on its banks. I see them float paper boats on it and run along. I look at the gutter again—and this time it is with a child's eye, and I can see only a river . . .

I walk away. I feel good. That is all that matters. The river takes a dying gasp and slinks away . . .

HOW TO BE
A NEWS EDITOR
Lung power—Shout/ Got lungs
Always be angry
Threaten to nuke
Pakistan every day
Dress for the occasion—
wear a spacesuit if India
is going to the moon
Don't get
distracted by facts

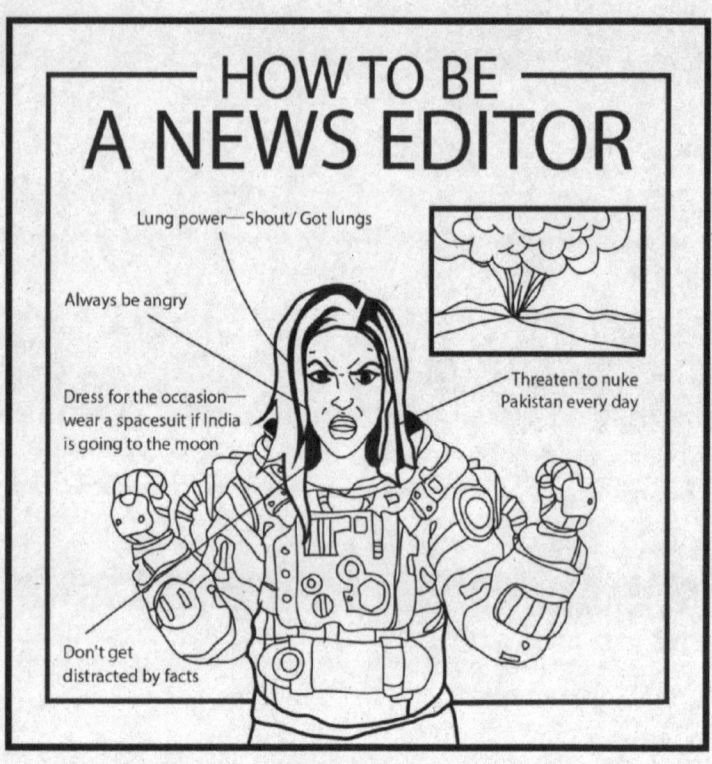

11

How to Be a Journalist and Never Report on Anything

I can anticipate what you are expecting here. You expect a reference to Noam Chomsky. He is the usual done to tedium suspect. Chomsky is the apostle of many a precocious journalism student and who with Edward S. Herman co-wrote the seminal *Manufacturing Consent: The Political Economy of the Mass Media* thirty years back. The book has had many revisions since 1988 and has sold millions of copies. What Herman and Chomsky famously said amongst many things was that the media could not afford to question power by virtue of its corporate ownership and its dependence on advertising. Therefore, the myth of a free and fair media was just that—a myth. In reality, media was a by-product of market forces and it made sense for it to play along with the powers that be. Therefore, at best, the media was a status quoist and at worst, a propagandist. And it toed the line without explicit coercion. I see you are perplexed. You have no idea who or what Chomsky is. Save yourself the trouble of doing an Internet search for him. His views are absolutely irrelevant to the scheme of this book. You have passed an important test—you are the ideal reader for this book.

We can now cheerfully proceed with the true objective of journalism, which is to make sure we stay in a bubble of self-involved knowledge. We choose to know only that much that suits us. And that is where later thinkers say Chomsky and Herman might have erred a bit by assuming that the reader/news consumer doesn't know—it is more likely he or she chooses not to know. We have already established in previous chapters that what we think is truth is often just a validation of our own belief systems. What we seek then is the post truth, which is a bit like the after-party once verified facts have left the party. It is where the real fun begins. Post truth is defined as a situation where people accept arguments based on emotion rather than objective standards for truth. It is usually found in abundance on a very credible broadcast medium—WhatsApp. But even conventional media rightly plays to the demand to show truths that have an emotive appeal. It is what the consumer wants. And if you don't give it to them, they will find it on tailored newsfeeds on Facebook and you will be redundant.

Now, if you are a journalist or an aspiring journalist, you will thank me for how adroitly I have eased your conscience by putting the onus for credible news on the consumer. Though, it is slightly silly to have had a conscience in the first place, but I won't get judgemental. A rather quaint description of the media is that of it being 'the fourth estate' (the other three estates being the legislature, the executive and the judiciary). As a media practitioner, you were traditionally then expected to ask counter-questions on matters of polity, governance and commerce. Which is why your superfluous conscience might be a tad burdened by this lofty job description—but you really need to do no such thing. Your consumer doesn't want you to, your media owner doesn't want you to and your news editor definitely doesn't want you to. In fact, most news editors, especially in television, hardly know you exist. You are just a pair of hands that can construct sentences with barely adequate grammar. If you are slightly brighter and ambitious, that could extend to writing click-bait headlines. But don't stretch yourself beyond that. I repeat—you really don't need to.

If you still, however, feel this romantic desire to ask counter-questions, here is how you can squash it. Stay away from multiple or conflicting facts. Accept things at face value. Let's do this step-by-step. How will you possess yourself of multiple facts? Well, you could start with reading up—that is secondary fact aggregation. You could do that, but always be selective in the facts you pick to retrofit to your preordained narrative. Preordained by your editor who thinks he is God. And it is very likely He is. But even selective aggregation is actually a lot of work, so I suggest you go with your gut and instinct. Completely infallible and something you have full control over. Now, you could have a temporary bout of insanity and go a step further in this noble mission of fact accumulation. You could actually step out into the world and report from the ground. But never do that—especially if you eventually want to be a news editor. A news editor brings multiple opinions, not facts, together and if he or she is in television, shouts over all of them. Facts and ground reportage should ideally not enter the picture at all. They will sober things down and spoil the party. Enjoy the cacophony of democracy. Facts are like the stuffy, authoritarian librarian who wants you to read in a corner and keep silent. Strike them off your list.

So now you have only one set of facts to go with— that makes your life easier. That is the only version you will bandy on television, print or the Internet. As a journalist, it is your business to keep tabs on the popular pulse and make sure the set of facts you have picked are in sync with that. News must give the viewer or the reader an emotional high. News must entertain and engage, and if it manages to inform, then that we must treat as unfortunate collateral damage. We really don't want to inform anyone of anything at all. We want to keep journalism as minimal mind work. But you will have to camouflage your mental inactivity with frenetic physical activity. That, unfortunately, is non- negotiable. You have to *look* charged up and bursting with zeal when you are anything but that.

For the purpose of conceptual clarity, I would like to give you customized slacker guides for different kinds of journalism. We will start with the most high-profile and glamorous kind—television journalism. Here is how you can be a star on television news without ever doing a single half-decent investigative report or unearthing any kind of scam.

1. Be loud, be excitable, be a superhero. Television news is not for the feeble-hearted or the feeble-voiced. Be loud. Remember, we are part of a culture where noise is synonymous with productivity. We do things loudly in this country—we work loudly, we talk loudly, we fight loudly, we grieve loudly and we celebrate louder than all of these put together. Therefore, when we see a news anchor being loud and decisive on TV, we are conditioned to believe that he or she knows what they are talking about. If the anchor is reasonably excitable too, his or her credibility goes up proportionately with the decibel level. A crash course in theatrics or a drama workshop will boost your career—it will teach you how much to raise your voice, where and when to take a pause and the right body language. Practise in front of a mirror every day. Glower. Bellow. Shake your fists. Peer. Flare your nostrils. Role play. Be a superhero.

2. Your superpower is anger. You have to figure out a way of staying angry all the time. Give up on yoga,

meditation and chanting classes—you don't need inner peace. The world needs you to stay angry. You also don't want the world to have peace—you will lose your job. Work yourself up into a vigilante anger, ask furious questions. However, note that your furious questions are never to be directed at figures of authority. Line up some inconsequential spokespeople, throw in a few out-of-work army generals from Pakistan and bellow. Be righteous and emotional in your anger—your prime-time meltdown is cathartic for your viewers. As you verbally pummel your equally angry panellists, the appetite of your audience is whetted for the next season of *Big Boss*. If on the off chance you do manage to get an interview with a genuinely powerful person, ask them which variety of mango they like to eat. The nation, I assure you, will want to know.

3. Be nationalistic. An important requisite for a television news editor is patriotism. These brave souls place the country above everything—especially independent investigation and verification of news. What these gallant men actually want to do is stand at the borders and lead marauding troops into enemy territory, but unfortunately, much against their will, they instead have to lead things from the hostile terrains of cushy, air-conditioned studios. These intrepid men refuse, though, to be cowed down by their comfort. They constantly call for and threaten war. Sometimes

they dress for the occasion too; only too often, you will find news anchors dressed in combat fatigues, especially when things are a bit tense with our pesky neighbours. Such heroic, swashbuckling men— let's not tell them the only people wearing combat fatigues when not in the army are teenage girls.

Do remember that the narrative of 'the national interest' will always take precedence over everything. In a chapter called, 'The Fear That Binds' in his book *The Power of Others*, writer Michael Bond talks about how a month after 9/11, 'George W. Bush achieved the highest approval rating of any president on record, over ninety per cent [. . .] and cut right across political boundaries.' A powerful cocktail of fear and national interest 'helped them (the Republicans) win the popular backing they needed for the war against Saddam Hussein despite no credible evidence that he had anything to do with Al -Qaeda's attacks on New York and Washington'.

Ace this game then—if you can make actual reportage and fact-gathering seem like an anti-national activity, you can continue to loll around in your studio for the rest of your career shouting down divisive forces. The biggest bonus to this is that you will come across as a national hero. Without ever actually doing anything at all.

4. Be a spectacle. As a culture, we like spectacles. We like things to be larger than life. We are not that

interested in the story if the spectacle can hold our attention. Confuse and visually distract your viewer— twenty people speaking in twenty little windows on your TV screen. All at once. Animated thumbnails jousting for attention. Add screaming graphics and hashtags. What are the chances that the viewer will catch on to the fact that you actually have nothing of insight to say? It is an old trick in soap television that television news has co-opted. Dizzying camera angles, abrupt zoom ins and outs and add to that, an anchor sprinting across the studio floor with his legion, breaking news by the micro-second. Place your viewer on a relentless roller coaster of breathless nonsense. The credulous will lap it up, the discerning will lay it on thick with snark on Twitter. But you have had the last laugh—you have managed to keep both watching and totally distracted.

The above should set you up for a fairly heady stint in television news, but if you are camera shy, it is easy to slack off in other forms of journalism too. In print journalism, which keeps asking for contributions to stay alive, all you need to do is write opinion pieces. Write an opinion piece, then get someone else to write a counter opinion piece, and then counter that opinion. All of this can be done sitting in your pyjamas at home. It is that easy. When it comes to digital and Internet news, the above model can be amplified to the power of infinity.

But in digital journalism an important weapon of mass distraction is the listicle. The listicle has killed more real news than Donald Trump's tweets. This is the lovechild of the Internet and cost-cutting newsrooms. It gives you engaging bunkum in easy-to-read, list format. Listicles require no research at all and can be spun out of anything. Throw any word at me. I will give you a listicle. Okay. Here goes. Let's take onion pakoda or bhajiya as it is called in Mumbai. Time me.

1. Five Times You Ate an Onion Pakoda All Wrong
2. This Onion Pakoda is Literally the Shape . . . of the Map of Gujarat
3. Americans Eat Onion Pakoda for the First Time. What Happens Next . . .
4. Modi Tells Indians to Set up Pakoda Stalls—5 Iconic Bhajiya Places in Mumbai

It is that easy. Fill the Internet and your working hours with this. Distract yourself and distract your reader. It is a double whammy.

If you are a business journalist in any medium, restrict yourself to reproducing press releases that companies throw your way. As a business journalist, your job is primarily to tell people how much money everyone is making and how it is all good. If you are an entertainment journalist, you are actually in limited peril and at the bottom of the value chain. Media companies have long figured that the best way to add some rupees to the bottom line is by converting entertainment news into paid advertorials. That reduces your role considerably, as that finally makes you a copywriter for a paid piece. It also means you won't ever get paid too much. It is a transaction—no one needs your networking or access. But if the objective is to slack off and not really report on anything of consequence, it is not a bad deal. And you do get to do the investigative stuff as well. After all, someone's got to tell the world about the five times Kareena Kapoor repeated her yoga pants to the gym and how that makes her just like us.

On that happy note then, post this on your Insta as your motivational post for the day: 'The function of journalism is primarily to uncover vital new information in the public interest and to put that information in a context so that we can use it to improve the human condition.' (Joshua Oppenheimer.)

And then write a listicle on 'Five Outdated Quotes on Journalism'.

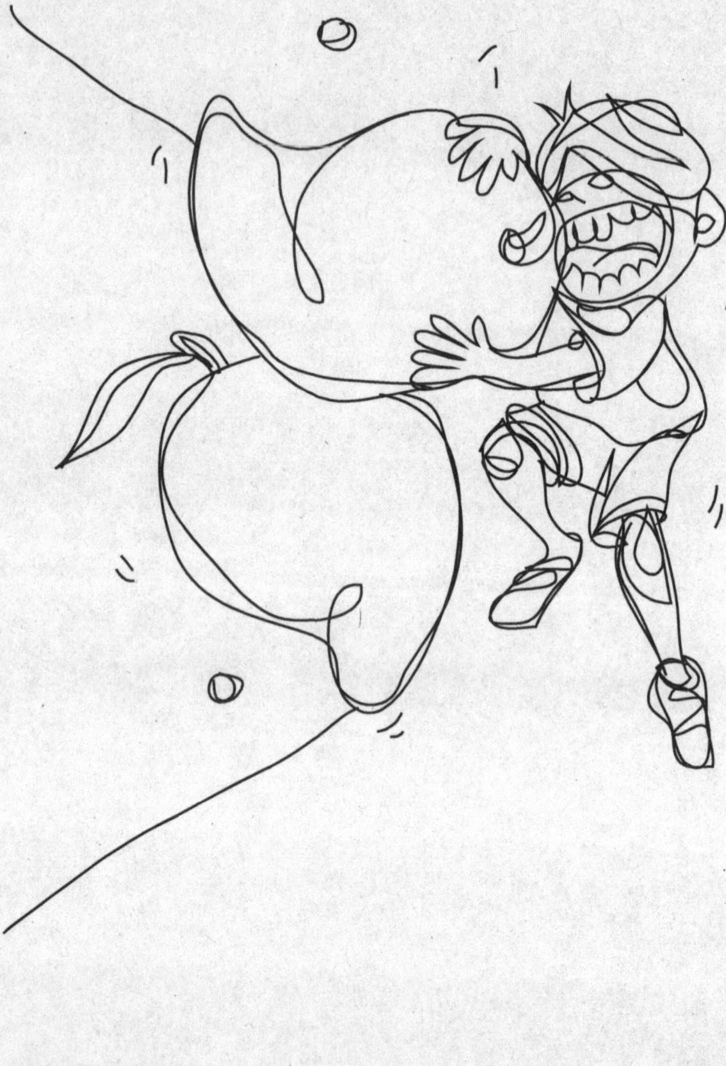

12

How to Crack Woke Jokes

The origin of the word 'woke' (if you do a quick Internet search) goes back as far as the eighteenth century. Being woke was and is associated with the black community and racial inequality. But in the present day, with heightened social media use, it has also come to mean a heightened state of social awareness—a relentless, joyless and often humourless quest for correctness. Very simply, it is political correctness on steroids.

It is a millennial thing too; if you are a millennial, you are likely to be more woke than a baby boomer or Gen X or Gen Z. A baby boomer would regard 'woke' as an incorrect usage of English. Gen X would find it an incorrect usage of English and deeply pretentious, and Gen Z will put it down as a fuddy-duddy relic—like television.

Being woke is looking at everything through filters and through the prism of social awareness. These are people who are weighed down by the sins of their ancestors and are only too aware of their privilege and entitlement. They find it difficult to opine, censure, gossip, joke, flirt or even react to simple things without being ridden by overarching guilt. Everything seems wrong if you put it in some kind of context. Every action or expressed opinion of yours has the ability to cause distress to someone else, and, therefore, you will find yourself incapable of action. This then is a state of hyper-activism that incapacitates you into a state of hyper-passivity. Perfect.

So why do we have this chapter in a book that is about maintaining the status quo? How does being a hyper-activist help our cause of making sure everything remains exactly the same and we get by with minimum effort?

Well, there are woke people—people who have fought for race equality and justice, bless them, but we don't care about them in this book. What we do care about is the social media version of woke. Let's call it Woke 2.0 and that is the wokeness we are going to focus on. Being this kind of woke means you don't really need to do a thing; you just get by saying the correct things. You are not a hyper-activist as much as you are an energetic slacktivist. (I asked you to google this aeons back.)

The advantages of coming across as woke are many: people assume you are evolved, sensitive and your conscience is alive and kicking. You might be uptight, a party pooper, a boring over-thinker, but your heart is in the right place. You are also fairly harmless because you won't really do anything. Doers are the problem. Thinkers are also a problem. But mental masturbators never are.

So how do we get you started on being woke? Well, since there is a lot of talking involved, the first thing we need to do is get you a 'wokeabulary'—a vocabulary with the right words.

Entitlement: This is the most important word that you need to bandy. You are intensely aware of your entitlement. It eats away at the core of your entitled being. You are even more aware of the entitlement of others. This is how you can weave this word into everyday discourse.

Example:

Friend 1: I love mangoes. They are my favourite fruit.

Friend 2: I think they are hugely overrated. Apples any day.

Woke you: I do hope you guys realize how entitled we are—that we can discuss mangoes and buy them. Seventy per cent of the people in this country have never bought a mango or know what it tastes like. (You can make up statistics. Nobody is checking.)

Friend 1: So we shouldn't eat mangoes? What is your point?

Woke you is unable to speak as currently your mouth is stuffed with a piece of mango.

Friend 2: Eat it, but just feel guilty about eating it?

Woke you: If you can't acknowledge your entitlement and want to be facetious, there is no point of this discussion.

(Friend 1 and 2 lose their appetite and you get to eat their share of mangoes as well.)

So while you acknowledge your entitlement, it will not come in the way of a whole-hearted consumption of the said mangoes. You just have an intense self- awareness of your privilege all the time. It is like travelling in business class but fretting about how limited leg space could lead to deep vein thrombosis in economy for others. It is about a physical body that travels club class, and a conscience that travels cattle class.

Privilege: This is the Bonnie to the Clyde of entitlement. Privilege goes hand in hand with entitlement. Privilege is the excess baggage of the affluent. I would advise you to enjoy your privilege if you have it—but if you do want to posture, this is the right book for you.

Example:

Commuter 1: These guys burning buses and holding up traffic are criminals.

Commuter 2: These guys should be in prison.

Woke you (sitting at home active on FB): This is an outpouring of years of systemic, wilful neglect and if you don't get what is at the core of this, consider that your privilege speaking.

Privilege is like God. He or She is omniscient, omnipotent and ominous.

You can find privilege in any and everything, in similar situations or in completely contrasting situations. If a person does not vote, that is a privilege. If a person votes, that too is a privilege. Privilege is also like a potato; it fits in well anywhere.

Agency: Don't be daft—agency isn't what you think it is. It isn't an agency like an advertising agency or a cooking gas agency. Agency, in this context, 'is the capacity of individuals to act independently and to make their own free choices'. We could have simply called it free choice, but agency just sounds deeper. How do you use it? Try and use it in the context of women; it will get you many brownie points. Women and agency are together a thing.

Examples:

1. Dating apps give women agency—they are now in a position to negotiate their choices in a free-market love economy. (They might just be in it for casual hook-ups, but let us not say that.)
2. Giving women agency is what is at the crux of this issue. (It doesn't matter what the issue is, just say this each time.)

Also, always remember to interlink agency with the dismantling of patriarchy. In fact, anything you do as a woke person only helps bring down patriarchy. Turning vegan, Pilates, a handstand—they all bring down patriarchy.

Joke: A joke is something that doesn't exist for a woke person. Humour by its very nature is at the expense of something or someone. That something or someone is now under the WPA—no, not the Witness Protection Act but the Woke Protection Act. You cannot make women jokes, men jokes, gay jokes, non-vegetarian jokes and definitely no Santa Banta jokes. Humour in the woke world is like a vegan joke: bland. If you are woke, you have lost your ability to find anything remotely funny. So let us safely assume that as a woke person, you have no assortment of lame jokes, sex jokes or any manner of puns. You just cannot make a joke. It is against your conscience. It feels illegal.

So you can't be funny—but what can you laugh at? Here is the trick: you don't laugh because a person is humorous. You laugh because the person is doing some sort of course correction for humanity. For instance, a woman comedian. She could be genuinely funny, but you are there to support her because you have to make up for generations of women who never had the chance to be funny. It is a bit like the diversity quota—'Ah, that lady just said something that was not funny, but let me laugh along, because I have to make up for my mum's generation, which never stepped out of the kitchen, let alone cracked jokes.' And the only reason you should find this reference to women even mildly amusing is because it is written by a woman.

Actually, no jokes on diversity quota—or any kind of quota. You know the drift—entitlement, privilege, the works. Therefore, as a woke person, you don't actually have to look for punchlines and humour to laugh. Look for how a joke is setting things right, how it represents a movement and how it empowers and uplifts something or someone. Only then should you allow yourself a discreet giggle. You never really throw back your head and laugh, because that is insensitive to people who don't have heads.

Our endeavour is humour with a conscience.

The 'ic' words: Other words that you should use liberally are endemic, systemic and problematic. Keep emblematic for special occasions. Problematic is the woke class-topper. You can't be woke unless you use it for everything. You find everything problematic; the degree varies, the intensity may not be consistent, but everything finally is problematic.

But before we get too carried away—and because we don't ever want to get too intense or involved in anything—I suggest we keep away from hardcore topics like politics and religion to put a problematic skew on. We don't really want to go down that route. No room for conflict. We want to get out of this alive.

So here is the thumb rule: when it comes to putting a problematic skew on things in the public domain, pick a soft target. Pick mass culture. Pick Bollywood. Even the Karni Sena will endorse that; there is no easier target than Bollywood.

When you pick something to find problematic in mass culture, make sure it is cult or iconic. Don't pick *Golmaal*. Like duh. Pick *Dilwale Dulhania Le Jayenge*. *DDLJ*, like the other pet woke target, the sitcom *F.R.I.E.N.D.S.*, can be bashed on many levels. It upholds patriarchy. The woman has no agency. Raj has no concept of personal space when he first meets Simran. There is no diversity in the glut of Punjabiness: I couldn't find any Iyers or Raos or Lyngdohs. It slut-shames white women. It celebrates *karva chauth*. It glorifies Switzerland—thereby shaming

Ooty. It force-feeds pigeons. It shows you rich people—thereby celebrating privilege. It is the stuff of romance and it is just a supremely entertaining film; I don't know how that slipped in. Of course not. Everything else holds.

So that is quintessential woke behaviour. Pick a product from a few decades back and view it through contemporary filters and write Twitter threads on it. If you are a slightly more proactive woke person, write a blog.

Just remember: being able to actually enjoy something is the kryptonite to wokeness. Don't enjoy—anything.

You know how 'enjoy' is almost an Indian greeting—think of that random elder relative who after a few irrelevant questions says meaningfully, 'So, enjoying?' without specifying what you are enjoying, and yet you feel duty-bound to immediately get into a state of disconnected enjoyment. Being woke is the exact antithesis: you are duty-bound to never enjoy. Anything. Everything. Nothing.

Always be on your guard. We cannot let the forces of levity sneak up on us. Let a nagging sense of guilt be our only constant guide.

Don't go over to the light side.

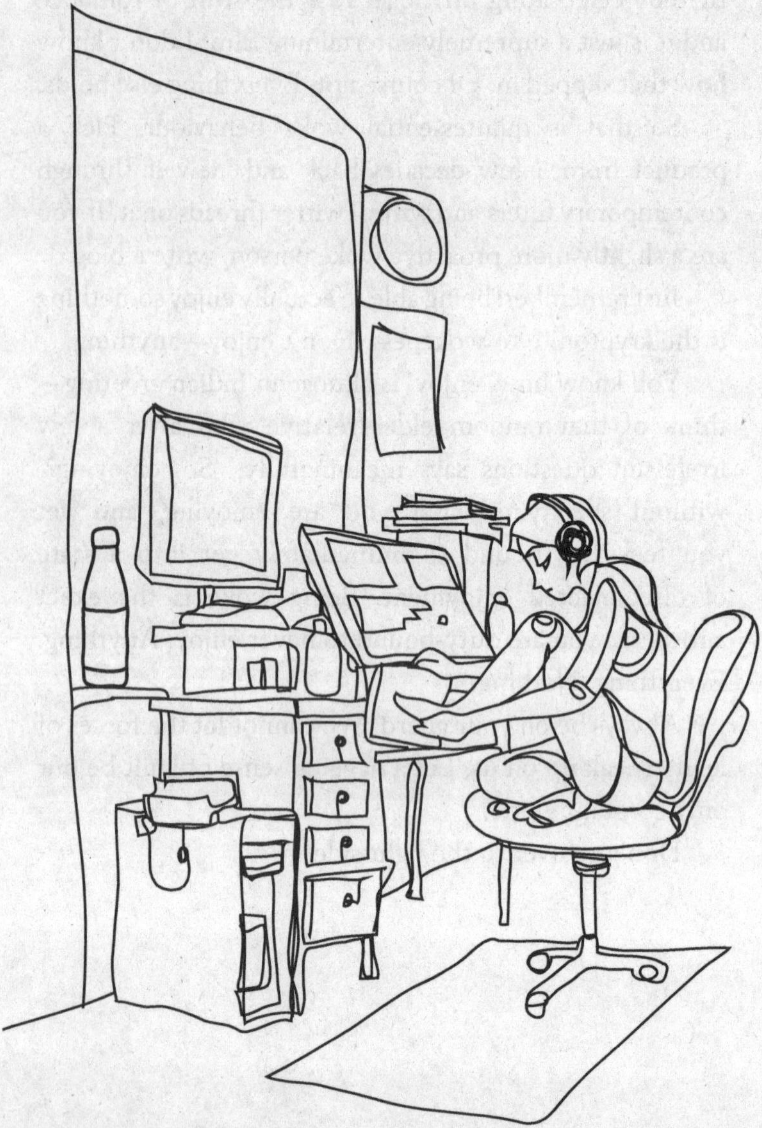

13

How to Be Casually Sexist

THINGS WOMEN ARE GOOD AT
(FROM THE MANUAL OF CASUAL SEXISM)

Looking good

Smiling

Shopping

Ordering lunch

Making lists

There are some ground rules that you need to internalize about women: they are excitable, emotional creatures driven by the dark forces of their menstrual cycles. They are moody, humourless control freaks whose prime objective is to get in the way of a boys' night out. They don't get cricket or football. They probably pretend an interest in sports to see athletic men drenched in sweat. Can you blame them though? No, don't tuck in that beer belly now. It is best to regard them as unidimensional cut-outs who either shop too much or talk too much. Let's not get too much nuance into our discussion of women—because, let's face it, you are possibly a man. Men don't get nuance, and it makes sense to live within your limitations.

In the last few years, men have been on the back foot. Pounded relentlessly by alpha women with that loaded M-word: Misogyny. Hyper-sensitive women have taken the fun out of flirtation, banter, stalking, sexual harassment and the odd date rape. You can't even make wife jokes without women showing up as party poopers dangling the sexism card. Where is all this pent-up anger coming from? Give or take an odd century or two or maybe more of systemic discrimination and repression, women have had it fairly easy. In another time and age, we could have asked men to be men and show women who is the boss. But now, men have to exercise caution and at least for the sake of appearances, rein in their masculinity.

It is only now that being traditional, old school, conservative or just old-fashioned is being clubbed under these umbrella definitions of 'patriarchal' or 'misogynistic'. Both are such misleading terms and overlook a basic tenet of human life, which is 'men will be men'. If things have worked well for a few centuries, and the human race is not extinct, surely it makes sense to keep things exactly the way they have been. But how do you balance it? How do you retain the masculine kernel of your forefathers and yet be socially acceptable to increasingly empowered women?

It is very simple: keep it casual. Keep it subtle. People have extreme reactions to extreme situations but not too many people get undercurrents and undertones. Be a casual misogynist; be the man your forefathers were. Just be matter-of-fact about it. Be urbane. Be suave. Be light. Don't change your tune. Just change your tone. Be non-toxic masculine. It is a lot more potent.

As usual, here is a step-by-step breakdown.

1. Always Complete Sentences for Women

Women go far too much into exposition and explanation. You, on the other hand, are pithy and precise. Keep completing sentences for women and constantly interject and speak on their behalf. The poor hapless creatures get so hassled by the use of words in a public space that it needs a man to step in and save them the blushes. It doesn't matter that by completing the sentence you are completing the thought that you probably have no idea about. Don't let your lack of domain knowledge stop you. You are a man. You were born to wing it. But do this respectfully: do it with empathy as if you are a good listener aiding a conversation. It doesn't matter if you haven't heard a thing of what they are saying. Just help them say it. That's what men do.

2. Always Explain Things to Women

Women don't get things. Men have to step in and have a ready reckoner on hand. In another era, this would be called chivalry, but modern chroniclers defame it as 'mansplaining'. This is far too facetious and flippant a term for good old-fashioned gallantry. Men know that women don't want their pretty little heads bothered with too many details, so they step in and explain stuff. However, so that you can avoid accusations of 'mansplaining', always seek permission from the lady in question to explain her ideas. Something like this:

As a result of her gender, the woman is largely not saying anything worth listening to.

You (your tone has to be the right mix of encouragement and condescension): That is a great idea. If I could just sum it up?

Lady: Uh . . . (Rule 1—Never let her complete her sentence. She is flailing. She needs your help.).

You neatly step in and explain her idea back to her and anyone else who might be in the vicinity.

Make sure your sexism has oodles of magnanimity. At every stage of this alleged 'mansplaining', make sure to preface it with 'like you were saying' and 'like you pointed out' and then happily expound further. The lady in question will be grateful to have your powers of clarity and concision and appreciate your generosity in acknowledging her idea and giving it credit. Also liberally drop in 'correct me if I am wrong'. Most women are not conditioned to correct male behaviour and so you are safe. You will not be corrected. On the rare occasion that you are, the woman will come across as unduly aggressive or belligerent. It is always win-win for you. And it isn't your fault. You are just of the right gender. You didn't choose to be. It happened. Deal with it. Be a man.

3. Don't Break Stereotypes; It Saves Thinking Time

Let us make a pact. Let us not try and change stereotypes. We don't want to bring about upheaval; it is incredibly inconvenient. Especially when it comes to women, stereotypes must always come into play. Psychologist Madeline E. Heilman of New York University in a paper on workplace sexism spoke about how women are often at the receiving end of two kinds of stereotyping: descriptive stereotyping and prescriptive stereotyping. Let me man up and explain this to you further.

You put a woman in a largely male workforce, assess her for a role that is a traditional male domain and then use gender attributes to gauge her 'fit' as opposed to her individual attributes. We don't know about her ability, but we attach 'feminine traits' to her—caring, emotional, pacifist. It is quite easy then to see that she is not cut out for a role that needs 'masculine' attributes such as aggression and logic. Therefore, end result: incompetent. That is descriptive stereotyping.

On the other hand, if a woman gets the job and now behaves like a 'man'—she is aggressive, combative and hard-nosed—it is again a problem. This now is in violation of traditional behaviour norms for women. Clearly, she is out of control and not fit for the job. Therefore, end result: incompetent. This is prescriptive stereotyping. Either way, the woman doesn't make the cut. A large part of this kind of stereotyping can be the use of the phrase, 'for a girl'. She is tough 'for a girl'. She is good at coding 'for a girl'.

You can, however, pass this off as admiration—and it is admiration. Only overwrought feminists would overthink this; ignore them.

Did you ever imagine that stereotyping could have so much nuance to it? There is no reason for us to therefore abandon it. You must contribute to it in your own way—in small, subtle ways. When you go out for a team dinner, ask the woman to order the meal because that's what women do—order meals. If some task requires paperwork and follow-up, ask your female colleague to do it. Women are better at administration. You, on the other hand, are the ideas person. If you have a female boss who is controlling and combative, it has nothing to do with her individual ambition and personality type. She is a female boss gone rogue and a bitch. There is good reason why women can't deal with leadership roles. Snicker about it and wonder if she has an inactive sex life, which is leading to pent-up aggression at the workplace. Chances are your female colleagues will also join in. They believe in the stereotype as much as you do. Perhaps even more. They could be your closest allies. Co-opt women in your casual sexism; they are believers.

4. The Only Context for Women Is Men

Women should never be judged on their own terms ever. The only context for them is their relevance to men. Women are assessed through the male gaze and that is the filter of approval or disapproval for their behaviour. Male actions are gender neutral: their sex is not the driving force. Female actions are always about gender: their gender is the motivator. Sounds fair. Which is why if a man is a victim, it is about what the perpetrator did. But if a woman is a victim, it is about what the victim did. Again, sounds completely fair. Never lose sight of clear-headed logic like this.

As a man, you are well within your rights to expect women to behave in a way that makes you comfortable. However, you are under no such corresponding obligation: your behaviour has no such caveats. You know about the 'bitch face' mode? Men don't have 'bitch face' mode. Only women who have to be perennially smiling and pleasant have it. Women must be dressed in a way that doesn't tempt men. Men have no onus not to get tempted. Our ecosystem is actually quite pro-women; it operates on the belief that men cannot be changed or redeemed. Therefore, the onus is on the women to save the men from themselves. Which actually puts women in a position of power: they have the power to govern male behaviour. Men, on the other hand, clearly can't be expected to exercise self-control. Therefore, the only context and relevance for women can be how they control men. They cannot abdicate responsibility by not behaving in a way that makes men behave. It would be irresponsible. There is no harm, therefore, in perpetuating a system that gives women . . . agency. Case closed.

In conclusion, you do realize that there is nothing casual about casual sexism. It is subtle, subliminal and nuanced. You have to work on it. You have to hone it to a fine art. Anyone can be a chauvinist. Any dullard can be a misogynist.

But casual sexism needs craft. Persevere and it will soon come naturally. Internalize all the principles discussed above and after a bit, you won't even have to try.

14

How to Be a Sports Legend without Ever Getting Injured

Few things excite humanity more than the spectacle of sporting effort. This is the laboratory of amazing feats that the human body and psyche can achieve—promoting the professional sportsperson to the ranks of the human race's physically elite. These meta-humans, honed through physical rigour and sculpted in the heat of competition, have the fixated attention and admiration of billions. This frenzied adulation used to be a phenomenon that was earlier only reserved for kings, emperors and demigods. The leaping, throwing, hitting, tumbling, thumping, twirling and gliding of sports stars now dictates the heart rate of people around the world, rapt in fandom. We kneel in worship.

Sports, which was once a childish amusement and preoccupation, is now the central activity around which we organize our lives and risk driving accidents when we peek at the latest score update. Sure, there are studious homebodies who dis this obsession with mass frivolity because it robs more noble pursuits, such as discovering a cure for cancer or reducing the rate of infant mortality, of money and attention. But have they considered the many lives that sports has helped save? Who can deny that hundreds of hulking, unemployable young men who spent more time lifting metal than studying it weren't saved through the sports quota? Who can refute the fact that millions of involuntarily celibate engineering students have been kept sane by using India's cricketing calendar to add meaning to their lives? And how can we forget the masses of paramedical staff and astrologists that are now gainfully employed thanks to the sprouting of various sporting leagues for everything from kabaddi to thumb-wrestling.

The modern-day sportsperson has us awed: he or she is the almost magical culmination of endless practice, parental obsession and sublime skill and stamina. Equally, the potent combination of marketing, brand endorsement, broadcast deals and social media have made the modern-day athlete, already bulging in physical proportions, even larger than life. Just as well. After all, these icons cut across all strata of society and give people something to bond over, despite having nothing of substance to say to each other.

Now, no series of childhood dreams is complete without at least one episode being devoted to sporting glory. But when all the coaching classes have been attended, expensive sporting gear worn and minor competitions braved, most of us are going to come to the crushing realization that an MBA is likely to lead to a greater chance of gainful employment. Sporting implements quietly set aside, remote controls firmly gripped, we will seek solace in watching televized sports and reflect on what might have been. Some of us may even thumb through the odd sporting biography. The more enterprising amongst us will even organize parties to watch a crucial match with our unabashedly unathletic friends and acquaintances. And just like that, we will fail to see the glorious sporting future that still awaits us. In our despondence over not captaining the country's cricket team, kicking our way to the golden boot or streaking across the Olympic track, we will throw in the towel, receding to couch potato oblivion.

Well, not all of us.

Some of us can still be the stuff of sporting legend—without moving a muscle.

Some of us can still dare to dream. Stay the course; we will tell you how.

What drives the sporting heroes of our age to their mythical status isn't merely the worldwide telecast of their feats or the communal gathering to watch their heroics. It is also the devotion of the unsung sports fanatic who has ventured on a cerebral journey through sports history. This is a species of great intrepidity and courage. After years of failed effort at actual sporting prowess, this invisible sporting hero has been both propagandist and performer, patron and passionate supporter. He is oft shushed, sometimes sought after, but always audible. His extraordinary command of sporting secrets from the ages, his willingness to plumb the ancient data tables of league statistics, his ability to number crunch during the strategic timeout have taken on mythical proportions. Meet this repository of purely useless sporting information: the Sports Geek, an unheralded hero of our times.

Here is the thing about this sporting hero: he is armed with voluminous data, which he rattles off faster than a Jasprit Bumrah delivery. But there is no insight or strategy that he brings to the table—a fact he hides well in the sheer volume of data he throws your way. So he becomes the stuff of legend. 'You know Arvind?' you say in tones of admiration, 'he really knows his sport'. And suddenly, the aforesaid Arvind is on hallowed ground without ever having stepped on a sporting ground.

Are sporting heroes born or made? That is the perennial question that experts across the ages have tried to answer. This question first sprouted in the training rooms of actual athletes. As state-sponsored programmes sought to imply world dominance through sporting ascendancy, the Americans, Russians, and inevitably, Chinese, devoted millions of dollars and scientific endeavour to answering this question. At stake was national pride, political propaganda, command of the world's imagination and ideological supremacy.

Till today, competing theories have rallied behind the 'nature versus nurture' argument that has echoed through scientific symposiums and beer bars alike. Is Jamaica's utter dominance of the track and field speed events the legacy of the slave trade where the fastest and strongest were bred? Certainly the parentage of Usain Bolt and the legendary clutch of Jamaica's track stars would suggest it. But then how does one explain the fact that tennis' global superstars have followed no pattern linked to lineage or racial origin? Neither have several of today's superstars necessarily come from genetic stock that belonged to sporting dynasties. Sure, having a parent or family member in professional sports raises your chances of being a professional sportsperson by a thousand per cent relative to a regular person. But all greatness begins somewhere and even genomic research has barely managed to isolate the 'sports gene'. All we know is that legends emerge from seemingly nowhere. The Sports Geek is a similar phenomenon. He too, like the comic book superhero, is a lone wolf and a solitary crusader who emerges out of practically nowhere. Armed with statistics, anecdotes and curious conflations, he strides alone. However, there are a few identifying characteristics of this legend that you can emulate if you want to follow in his footsteps.

The Sports Geek follows but one rule and one rule only: no matter what, no matter how, no matter the threat of pain or punishment, NEVER PLAY SPORT.

This is key. Not for this sporting legend are the toils of the field or the exertions of the gym. His work is of the mind, the intellect, and that refuge of all those incapable of original thought, the Internet. Ever ready to perform mental calisthenics, cerebral gymnastics and the massaging of statistics, Sports Geek demonstrates his unique command of sport, any sport. If you thought that playing a sport gave you a sense of its difficulty or the impossibility of the skills displayed by its best, you stand corrected. With little or no real experience and even less effort, Sports Geek will demonstrate, through insightful, but ultimately inconsequential commentary, that mastery is a matter of information, not athleticism. Regard his command of the obscure factoid. Admire his grasp of the convoluted statistic. Ponder his weighty prediction of things to come based on tangential 'inside' information.

If you are befuddled by the mysterious ways of Sports Geek, take heart. We are here to break down his method and give you a measure of this strange being in human form. Let's place you in the middle of this battle of the mind. Picture this: India has just suffered a sudden and deeply saddening exit from the Cricket World Cup. Its warriors were the favoured few. Ascendant and all powerful, they demolished everyone in the league stages, but in the crucial moments of a decisive semi-final, stumbled when they needed to win the most. The weather, the Kiwis, a surprisingly fragile top order and a tepid bowling performance in the face of a defiant Kiwi team has resulted in a heartbreaking loss that has stunned a billion people. What follows are the usual recriminations, regret and the rueing of missed chances. The world's best weren't good enough on the day and now pubs all around the country will be left with the excess stock of alcohol they had purchased in anticipation of India making the finals.

It is at this crucial juncture that the bruised Indian fan in you will met the Sports Geek in his element. Sample his handiwork as he cocks a snook at the fallen heroes and the apologetic commentators.

First the throat-clearing, then the tone of intellectual superiority and now, the barrage of utterly useless facts to boggle the mind:

'Er, did you know that there is an uncanny resemblance in the fortunes of Australia and India, both favourites who exited the tournament?' (You didn't because you spent the whole week bemoaning their departure.)

'Really?' you inquire, half annoyed, half irate, but this escapes Sports Geek as he adheres to his low EQ stereotype. And now he launches.

'Well, India topped the league table and lost the semi-finals,' he chimes. (Er, yes, we are aware. Go on!)

'And Australia, who were following India, lost the semi-finals too,' he follows on enthusiastically. (Yes, this was all over the news. Everywhere.)

'Both countries end with an "ia" and countries ending in "land", i.e., England and New Zealand, are in the finals.' (Like we said, amusing, but completely useless.)

'Did you notice that India lost three early wickets and Australia also lost three early wickets?' (Yes, me and another billion people watching the telly did. Your point?)

'Dhoni got run out and Smith also got run out,' he continues unaffected and unable to detect sarcasm.

'Interestingly, Dhoni got run out when India were 216/8 and Smith got run out when Australia were 217/8!' he exclaims with an air of chin-tilting superiority. (But that's the previous fact with the team score added to it!)

'AND, did you know that seven batsmen scored a single digit score and four of them scored double digit scores for both India and Australia,' he proclaims triumphantly. (Combust spontaneously in frustration.)

Regard the handiwork of this uncommonly insightful specimen. Note his command of banal facts, expressed in the most odiously ordinary fashion. Facts, numbers and the alarmingly obvious said in the most tediously workmanlike fashion but draped in an air of cerebral prowess. The fact that none of this has anything to do with what actually happened or why it happened hardly matters. You've been sports-geeked. Still standing? It might be time to up the ante for Sports Geek and call upon all his geeky might. Sample this.

'You know the Wimbledon final between Federer and Djokovic?' (Yes, me and another gazillion people, but sure, enlighten me.)

'You know that Federer lost right? (Sighs deeply, cue head shake.)

Here it comes.

'But did you know that Federer won more overall points (218-204) . . . had a higher percentage of first serve points (79-74) . . . had a higher percentage of second serve points (51-47) . . . had a higher percentage of points at net (78-63) . . . had more break points (7/13 vs 3/8),' now he's panting in ecstatic delight as he heads into a crescendo, 'AND HAD MORE WINNERS (94-54)!'

You catch yourself wishing this sort of unchecked idiocy was an act of terrorism that allowed for indefinite incarceration of the perpetrator. Congratulations, you've been sports-geeked!

The Sports Geek's origins are not well documented but there are certain defining traits of this prototype. Not to stereotype or anything, but he will usually have a management degree. Unable to make a name in the real world of sports, this crop of numerate, literate and often celibate species is intent on claiming unattained glory by astonishing you with absolutely pedestrian dissections of world sporting events atomized into mundane factoids. With half a youth spent preparing for ascendancy of the corporate ladder, his adult life will be spent sliding around trying desperately to be significant in some other realm.

Should you desire to join the ranks of this breed of inquisitive nerds, the formula is a little known inversion of insight available only to a nerdy few. In his bestseller *The Captain Class*, sports writer, *New York Times* journalist and two-time fantasy baseball league winner Sam Walker mined the records of thousands of teams from around the world in over thirty-five sports categories to better understand success. He noticed that some teams managed freakish runs of success at the highest ranks of the sport and became legends in their own right, stamping their names into the history books forever. What causes this astounding winning streak, he wondered. Star players? Stacks of money? Cunning coaching? What he unearthed after twelve years of research would have gladdened the thumping heart of any Sports Geek. Not a little-known detail or an uncanny insight not obvious to the untrained eye. No. For the Sports Geek, only the glaringly evident will suffice. It was the captain.

This might seem apparent at the outset were it not for all the other possible factors that success is usually attributed to. Walker's true insight, however, came in the seven counter-intuitive qualities that made these captains outlandishly successful 'real athletes'. This list of virtues, however, is the photographic negative of what the Sports Geek embodies. Want to be a Sports Geek? Simple. Be the opposite of the legendary captains of yore.

Here now, for the first time ever, is the template to follow in stark opposition to any real sportsperson:

REAL ATHLETE	SPORTS GEEK
Doggedness	Gives up quickly and changes the subject if anyone questions the utility of obscure sports facts
Playing to the edge of the rules	Observes only one rule: never play sports
Practical individualized communication	Only pompous declarations to everyone in the living room or pub will do
Non-verbal displays	Only verbal displays of unwanted expertise
Regulating emotion	Only hysteric proclamations inviting no scrutiny
Leading from the back	Is the only 'thought leader'. Everyone else is not.
Courage to stand apart	Stands amongst the many Sports Geeks; assertions are not be debated.

So revel in the knowledge that greatness is not beyond you. The way of the Sports Geek is available to all ye who choose to wander into its domain. Should Sports Geek's daredevilry with decimal points beguile you? Or should you seek to outdo the real athlete who has expended his adrenaline and melted his mitochondria in the quest for sporting glory? Your wait is over and your prize entails the painless, ego-enhancing endeavours of the Sports Geek.

In his seminal work *The Sports Gene*, which tries to answer the question we began with, 'Are sports legends born or made?', sports scientist David Epstein points out an intriguing experiment. He declares that athletes have indeed become faster. The reasons for it, though, might surprise us. An analysis of Jesse Owens in the 1930s versus Carl Lewis in the 1980s shows that the two athletes weren't actually very different from each other in terms of speed, once you adjusted for the environment. Owens was running on cinder tracks, which stole energy. Lewis, on the other hand, was running on synthetic tracks, which provided better traction. In much the same way that the surrounding technology has aided athletic performance, so too have the new implements of our age aided the ascendancy of the Sport Geek. With digital databases, self-anointed expert bean counters' blogs and professional WhatsApp forwarders providing ballast, the Sports Geek's utopia is already alive and fizzing with a fact a minute. Statistics are your steroids and the online repositories of sports punditry are your performance-enhancing drugs. The side effects: headaches, nausea, aneurysms. These are only to be suffered by your unwitting audiences, not you.

Come, wannabe Sports Geeks, dive, lunge and leap into the vortex of tangential trivia and revel in it even as you reach for your prized super bowl of chips on the couch. Sports heroes, Epstein ultimately declares, are the product of nature AND nurture. The two are inextricably linked.

Just like modern-day sporting glory and its ungodly illegitimate offspring, the Sports Geek.

15

How to Escape Reality and Live in a Parallel Timeline of Your Own

During my undergraduate years, I stumbled upon a line from a poem by T.S. Eliot: '. . . human kind cannot bear very much reality . . .' The line stayed in my head and is one of the most oft-repeated quotes attributed to Eliot. It is so common that it probably makes it to an existential coaster in a millennial coffee shop. The quotation is self-explanatory: human beings find reality difficult to handle. They'd rather get off the bus. But, we didn't get on the bus on our own, and we have no idea which is our bus stop, so we have to stay put till further notice. In case you haven't noticed, that is a pretty deep analogy on life and death. Just thought I'd point it out.

Anyway, we are now on this bus and the truth is that it really isn't what the tour operator promised. The ride is bumpy, the co-passengers can get a bit annoying and you can't help but notice the frayed, fading red of the seats. It started off with bold ambition but is now relinquishing its promise. You need a distraction device before the despondency swamps you. And then suddenly, there is in-bus entertainment—a screen in front of you lights up, a movie plays and you are transported into a narrative that takes your mind off the wretched bus. Your co-passenger is snoring and his elbow is in your space—but you have stopped noticing.

Soviet filmmaker Dizya Vertov in 1925 took what Karl Marx had said for religion and applied it to cinema to say 'the film drama is the opium of the masses'. This quote is more popularly paraphrased as another coffee-shop-coaster favourite, 'Cinema is the opium of the masses'. For a book that celebrates the status quo, we cannot overlook the singular impact of mass culture on maintaining it. It is our strongest ally. A strong factor in ensuring that all of humankind's role model is a potato.

Through my wonder years, television and cinema gave us periodic escapes from real life. If my parents' generation was about the smouldering anger of Amitabh Bachchan in a poor, socialist country, mine was about the insularity of newly wealthy India. I grew up on the staple cinema of the 1990s, where good-looking Indians spouting authentic Indian values fell in love with other good-looking Indians in countries that were very far from the heat and dust of India. Countries that had been purged of every foreign face except ours and where everyone strangely spoke Hindi. It was a curious la la land and we all wanted citizenship.

Our escapes, though, were weekly affairs, and the retreat into a parallel world was always meant to be short-lived. We were addicts, but ones who knew that our fixes would be doled out to us. And we still had to do the hard work of living most of our adult lives in mind-numbing drudgery and routine. There could be no perennial high.

But the human capacity to consume copious amounts of time doing nothing at all while deluding ourselves that we are in fact productively occupied cannot be underestimated. As the nothingness of life stretched out before us, we didn't find a cause to occupy us. We didn't think of making the world a better place to leave behind for our kids. We waited around for things to happen and they did. Netflix found us. Hollywood tracked us down with superheroes in spandex in franchise films. It all came fast and furious; we put up no resistance. We surrendered happily. There was no need to ever return now. We were in the world we wanted to be in. Real life retreated into the background, the lives of imaginary characters took over our every waking moment and our allegiance to them was now unshakeable. Binge-watching was now a hallmark of achievement, a badge of honour and probably the only endurance sport we knew.

To show our unswerving commitment to this alternative universe, we can go a step further on this never-ending joyride—we can join a 'fandom'. What exactly is a fandom? 'A fandom is a sub-cultural phenomenon composed of fans characterized by a feeling

183

of empathy and camaraderie with others who share a common interest'. That is the rather vanilla description. The common interest usually is a web series, a film, comic books or films based on comic books. Fandom is almost like being part of a cult, a commune of acolytes. Certain writers have said that it is like fanaticism; your commitment is as intense and involved as a right-winger's or a left-winger's but because it is to pop culture, it seems trivial. In other words, fandom is about being a pop-culture bhakt. Here is the thing: there have always been fandoms, but in another decade it would have been fringe—the reclusive comic-book geek spinning his own narrative around fantasy characters cut off from the mainstream. Now, it is a mass movement.

Fandom does not allow you to dismiss anything as 'just a film' or 'just a show'. That voice of sanity has been ruthlessly quelled. Because when you are part of a fandom, nothing is just a film. So what is it about Marvel, DC or even *Game of Thrones* that makes full-grown adults emotionally invest in that world? And why is the world turning into a massive fandom?

In his book *Slugfest*, which documents the epic fifty-year battle between Marvel and DC, writer Reed Tucker has an interesting take. He says Gen X and older millennials are the first generation not to outgrow comic books. That has a lot to do with the source material itself: 'The material has grown up. As a result, my generation became the first who didn't need to age out of superheroes.' There is a point in that. Look at the darker, grittier and overly adult tone that films from DC and Marvel have taken in the recent past. Comic-book fandom or franchise fandom now is a lifetime commitment. It isn't a 'life stage phenomenon' like say MTV or Cartoon Network, which you outgrow. Once you are in it, there is no getting out.

I have another take, and it is more relevant to what I hope to make of you by the time this book is done. Fandom is your outlet—from a world that is mundane, toxic or just jaded. It is so much more interesting to be invested in a narrative that has dragons, quantum realms, infinity stones and people in spandex. It is a world without Excel sheets, presentations and long commutes (unless you count time travel). It demands allegiance; it demands suspension of disbelief and an unwavering faith in an ideology. It gives you something to believe in, something to be passionate about, something to be vocal and strident about and it is so very easy. You don't really have to do a thing—and you don't need to think about the impending water crisis, the tanking economy or your toxic boss. Fandom means you are a vocal, articulate, opinionated tuber whose opinions will change nothing in the real world. Perfect. That is all we want.

Now, all we need to do is get you set up in a fandom of your own. A cozy commune of fellow human beings in the pursuit of nothingness. This is by far the most intellectual activity I am setting up for you—lest you accuse this book of deadening your intellect. Here is a complete guide on how you can ensure that the real world is but a blur, and all that matters is this one.

1. Find a cause. You cannot be wishy-washy on this one. Be a cause warrior—find the world that deserves you. It could be *Game of Thrones*, *Avengers* or *Naagin* (there, there—don't be a snob). Once you have found the world you want to inhabit, don't hold back. We may not want you to think too much, but we do need you to feel. Feel every twist, every turn in the plot; feel it intensely. Fight it out with other members of the commune: take sides, change sides, play musical chairs. Live in the constant intrigue of the world you have chosen.

2. Be in a position of knowledge. You cannot be a passive receptacle. Being part of this alternative universe needs time and effort. Be bleary-eyed trying to figure out what the quantum realm means based on a superhero film. Films, especially superhero ones that use the stock storytelling device of time travel, can often throw up many existential questions on the nature of time. Is time a loop or is it linear? It is probably just a tired script writer, but we will never say that. Be prepared to read a lot as you ponder and debate a film.

3. Reddit it. Don't be a novice. If you are part of a legit fandom, you now have to move beyond Twitter and Facebook. Reddit is where the action is, where

talented people like yourself are expending time and energy coming up with fan fiction and alternative narratives. You can spend hours, days and months here discussing stuff with your co-conspirators. You are probably unwittingly being used by the studios to fuel attention around their creations—but I wouldn't complain too much. At least this way you are of some utility to someone.

4. Binge-watching is your superpower. You have to be the first off the block. You will find reserves of inner strength that will take you through your gruelling marathon watch. It is a triumph of the human spirit that you can relentlessly sit in one place for eight hours at a stretch. Keep pushing yourself; set new benchmarks. Remember, you are your only competition. Don't let anyone tell you can't— because you can.

Following the above means that you will not need to talk to real people for the rest of your life. You will not dawdle in office, or take smoke breaks. You will do the bare minimum required to give you a salary, your marriage will be happy and you won't need to inflict your progeny on the rest of the world. You should occasionally video call your parents though. It is the very least you can do.

Retreat then into the parallel world of fandom. Soon it will be the only world that matters. This world is your oyster.

Select Bibliography

Books

Noam Chomsky and Edward S. Herman, *Manufacturing Consent: The Political Economy of the Mass Media* (Pantheon Books, 1988).

Michael Bond, *The Power of Others* (Oneworld, 2015).

Sam Walker, *The Captain Class* (Ebury Press, 2018).

Amy Chua, *The Battle Hymn of the Tiger Mother* (Penguin, 2011).

David Epstein, *The Sports Gene* (Yellow Jersey, 2018).

Anand Giridharadas, *Winners Take All—The Elite Charade of Changing the World* (Allen Lane, 2019).

Alan Miller and Satoshi Kanazawa, *Why Beautiful People Have More Daughters* (Penguin Random House, 2008).

Notes

Madeline E. Heilman, *Gender Stereotypes and Workplace Bias*, New York University, 2012.

Claire Fox, 'The Dangers of Illiberal Liberalism', *The Economist*, 2018.

Heather L. LaMarre, Kristen D. Landreville and Michael A. Beam, 'The Irony of Satire: Political Ideology and the Motivation to See What You Want to See', *The Colbert Report*, Ohio State University, 2009.

Acknowledgements

I wouldn't have written this book were it not for my publisher, Milee Ashwarya. It took eight years for the second book and she pretty much coaxed and cajoled the book out of me. Thank you, M!

If the book sometimes gives the impression that I am a well-referenced and well-read person—all credit to my husband, Adrian. He has a book and an accompanying podcast on everything. And I mean everything. He also coined the term 'kangaroo dad' and lives in hope that it will be the new 'tiger mum'.

My parents and my sister, Gopa. My father looks at the world in the same manner as I do—it never fails to amuse him. I reckon he gets it from me. My mum and my sister will be most miffed if I don't include them so here goes.

My WhatsApp groups especially *Very Senior Management* (V2 and Rony)—offline friends are overrated. We have the real deal. On a serious note, thank you for being a sounding board and not taking anything seriously ever. It is the only way to conduct our lives.

I do have offline friends—Harsha and Pallavi, thank you for being the best kind of friends. A completely approving support system!

Anita Balagopalan, Tina Tandon, Namrata Chawla Kapoor, thank you for all the insights on the trials and tribulations of modern mummyhood and the spectre of the birthday party. PS. Anita you are a terrible literary agent though.

Twitter friends, thank you for all the constant validation. It would be great if you could also buy the book now.

Staying with validation, a special note for my nursery school principal in Shillong, Mrs Bluebell Wasan. She pinned up my first story on the school noticeboard and a six-year-old realized she likes all the attention writing gets her. Thank you!